Charting the Heart of God Through Dreams & Visions

Charting the Heart of God Through Dreams & Visions

Rev. Dr. Barbara Sargent Green

Brandice Green Weathers, Ph.D

Charting the Heart of God Through Dreams & Visions

ISBN 979-8-9851441-2-3

Published by Conqueror Productions, LLC
Jacksonville, Florida

Table of Contents

Acknowledgments

This book is dedicated to my grandchildren, Braya Catherine Weathers, and Barrett Alexander Weathers. I pray that you dream dreams, see visions, and do great exploits for the kingdom of our God and the Lord Jesus! The mention of your names brings a smile to my face. Your Grandpa and I did not think we could be happier than when your mom was born and again after she got married. We were so wrong; first, Bevin came and brought us so much joy. Then you came along Braya, and you taught me "to be and not do." Following you, Braya, along came Barrett with his gentle spirit, and a constant smile. I see the peace of God upon you and my heart melts each time I see your beautiful smile. I have offered up prayers for both of you daily, and God has filled my nights with dreams concerning you.

On Sunday, March 15, 2020, during a time of chaos, fear and uncertainty in the world because of COVID-19, Braya delivered a profound and prophetic word to me. She had her mom call me and she said, "Grammy, I have something very important to tell you, I need you to do the right thing when God tells you what to do." This divinely inspired word from a 4-year-old has been a constant reminder for me to complete this book among so many other things while I was sheltered in during the COVID-19 season. I believe that this book is the right thing as I follow the prompting of God. I am amazed and in awe that the Lord spoke to me at that time through my 4-year-old granddaughter.

To my husband, Archie Jacob Green, Jr., the love of my life for almost 46 years. Your unconditional love and support have sustained me through three degrees and three pastoral assignments spanning 28 years and 33 years in ministry. Thank you for the many sacrifices you have made and never once complaining, which allowed me to engage in study and to lead congregations. Your listening ear and sensitivity to the Spirit of God allow you to know when to counsel and when to sit quietly and pray. To our one and only child, our daughter, Brandice (Brandi) Annette Green Weathers, God gave life to your dad and my love when you were born. For 44 wonderful years I have seen you blossom as a woman and mother who loves God, and your family. You and Dad have certainly been my cheerleaders. Brandi, you have encouraged me constantly by saying "Mom, you can do this." To my siblings, Cynthia, and Jerome Sargent, I love you.

To my parents, Jim O'Neil & Mary Anderson Sargent, both God have blessed to be dreamers and one who sees visions, thank you for being my "Dad and Mom." I praise God for praying parents. I have always felt your love. You reared me to be the person I am today. You taught us the value of family, to be truthful, and have integrity. Thank you for believing that I could do anything that I set my mind to do. Dad, I never realized how hard it must have been for you in the 60's to endure what you did while being one of only 2 Black Firemen and then to rise through the ranks to become the first and only African American to hold the position of Fire Chief for the City of Georgetown in South Carolina. You knew what it meant to push and never give up. It has been one of the things that has caused me to push through challenges in the ministry. Additionally, You and Mom made it your mission to be present at every major juncture in my life and have always been there to encourage me when ministry was difficult. Dad, you get to see "Sargent" in print again, first with my dissertation and now with this book.

I am also thankful to Cindy J. Schwartz, Ph.D. for writing the Foreword to this book. Cindy, you have been my Spiritual Director and the Project Director for my dissertation at Memphis Theological Seminary, (MTS).

Moreover, you have been a friend who challenged, pushed, and provided spiritual insight as I continued to write.

Next, I would like to thank my Presiding Elder, The Reverend Linda F. Thomas-Martin for her encouragement and support for almost 20 years. Thank you, Reverend Dr. Pearl L. Lurry and Reverend LaWanda Denise Pope, friends, and intercessors for giving me insight to interpret numerous dreams. Thank you Thelma J. Nelms, I had no idea when we met in 2006, that we would have had such a wonderful journey together. To Brenda Judkins and Joyce Cornelius (who I refer to fondly as Mary and Martha), thank you for your prayers throughout the years. To The Reverends Agnes Marie White Henderson, and Mary Hayslett, for being a sounding board along with your prayers and encouragement for over 25 years. Reverend Agnes your words resounded in my ears non-stop saying "Reverend Barbara at some point you must let it go." God has knitted our families together, and I am grateful to you and yours. Reverend Dr. Robin E. Henderson thank you for your gentle probing and for holding me accountable. To Nataline Purdy for working behind the scenes and for your words that made a difference in what I was doing. To Carolyn Wright Singleton, who was one of my high school teachers long before we became friends, thank you for the conversations reminding me that it will always be worked out by God, and to keep the faith.

Additionally, I want to thank Bishops Jeffrey N. Leath and Vashti Murphy McKenzie, former Prelates of the 13th Episcopal Church of the African Methodist Episcopal (AME) Church who have encouraged me and provided opportunities for me to share openly with them what God had given me through dreams.

Moreover, to Bishop E. Anne Henning Byfield, my current Bishop, thank you for your encouragement and inspiration by not only letting me know what I am doing pertaining to dreams and visions important, but that is needful because the work had not previously been done. Thank you for encouraging me to "Think Big" so rather than having a Dream Workshop, to have a Dream Conference and because of your foresight, in 2024, I will convene my 3rd Annual Dreamers Conference.

I praise God for The Reverend Dr. James E. Deas, Sr., my father in the ministry who transitioned on December 20, 2023. I am glad that I at least sent you some of what I wanted to say in the book while you were here on the earth. Reverend Deas you encouraged me to seek God more and not miss my personal devotion time with God. Reverend, you reminded me that my private devotion was my lifeline and foundation for my Doctor of Ministry project and everything else that I would ever accomplish in life. To Mrs. Ruth Davis Deas, you and Reverend Deas were always one. I am reminded that you were the one who gave me a book entitled "The Holy Spirit and His Gifts" by Kenneth Hagin in 1984 and you told me that God said two of the gifts that I had been given were "the word of knowledge and the word of wisdom."

To Reverend Dr. James Carter Wade and, Dr. Julia Revels Wade (who is in the presence of the Lord). Dr. Wade, God brought you into my life in 2006 as a second father in ministry at a crucial time during my current assignment. Dr. Julia, you were the older sister that allowed me to let my hair down. We sat at my dining room table, and you helped me think through what I said I wanted the project to be even though I could not see how it would work. You both have blessed me with your prayers and presence.

Additionally, I would like to say thank you to the staff of preachers (Reverends Marvette P. Miller, Alfreda T. Owens, Kimberly C. Ruguaru, Sisters Lottie Campbell and Laura Pounder and Brother Raymond Pounder along with the officers of Bethel (AME) Church in Memphis, TN. All of you stood in the gap, preached, and handled other responsibilities which afforded me the opportunity to complete my course work in the Doctor of Ministry (D.Min.) program at MTS and to write this book. I am blessed to serve as your Pastor.

To The Reverend Alfreda T. Owens, who volunteered in 2006 to be my armorbearer. I did not know how much I needed one. When you asked to be my armorbearer, my first response was I can carry my own purse and Bible.

In African American churches, an armorbearer could be a lay or clergy person. The role is analogous to that of an executive assistant as they provide for the need of the pastor while he/she performs pastoral duties. The armorbearer performs tasks that would divert the attention of the pastor, such as intercepting phone calls or drop-in meetings before the preaching moment. Reverend Alfreda, you have done so much more; you have sacrificed time to help pray for and with me even when I did not take the time or have the energy to pray for myself. I thank you for helping to pray me through the process while pursuing my D.Min., and taking on additional responsibilities that I did not know I needed to relinquish so that I would be less stressed. Thank you for not only praying for me and Brother Green, but you continue to pray for my parents, siblings, and our daughter, and her family as well.

Finally, I thank God and for all those near and far who prayed and cheered me on to follow the prompting of God. There are countless other people that remain unnamed. Thank you seems to be inadequate; you are too numerous to identify, but God sees and knows and will reward you accordingly.

I am most thankful to You; Holy Spirit for You have reassured me with your continued presence and the numerous confirmations along the way as I embarked upon this journey. My prayer is that God is glorified and that individuals are encouraged to pursue what God is revealing to them in their dreams and visions.

Foreword

By Cindy J. Schwartz, Ph.D.

When Barbara came to me with an idea for her dissertation, I was not surprised. It was already clear how deeply passionate Barbara was about the subject of dreams. For Barbara, the calling regarding dreams was like a fire that would not be quenched and she wanted to share the treasure she had received and continues to receive from God. It is a gift that she has already passed on to her daughter and granddaughter, who are a part of this book. Barbara did extensive research into the subject of dreams, interpretation of dreams in a Christian framework, and the practice of dream journaling. This text is less academic than her dissertation, but it is still full of the study and the life experience of its author.

Barbara synthesizes biblical passages and ties them to both concise comments regarding their connection to the different ways dreams can be beneficial in our formation as Christian, and she ties the Scriptures to examples of her own dream experiences. Then, having given many amazing stories of how God has used her willingness to listen to his dream gifts, the author goes on to end with practical suggestions for getting started in journaling and waiting upon the Spirit for discernment. She makes a powerful case that the practices of dream journaling and interpretation are faithful disciplines for those who follow Jesus.

On a personal note, this book came to me at just the right time, obviously God's timing. I was preparing to leave one call and move to another. The logistics and emotions of the transition were painful and sometimes confusing for me. Reading Barbara's faithful narrative on her own dreams and what followed was exciting and deeply moving. It provided encouragement and inspiration for this season of my life, because everything Barbara tells is refreshingly honest, and swirling with the wind of the Spirit's power. Every word she writes is real. No one more straightforward, for Barbara is an Israelite without guile (John1:47 ASV). If you know Barbara, this book is a small window into her beautiful soul. I am praying that it also meets the readers where there is need of encouragement or inspiration.

I am certain that Barbara has not poured out all she has to say on the subject of dreams. I am confident and hopeful that she will continue to explore and teach on this spiritual practice beyond this text. This, however, is a good start.

The Genesis of the Book

By Rev. Dr. Barbara Sargent Green

I am passionate about dreams and visions because this is one of the ways in which God has been connecting with me my entire life. I have considered my own exploration of dreams and visions and deepened my insight into the way that I have come to understand my relationship with God, who God is, and what God desires of me. The experience has been so revealing and meaningful for me personally and pastorally, that as my Doctor of Ministry project, I chose to examine how biblically and experientially dreams and visions are an integral part of our faith tradition. It is my contention that many persons have not been taught that dreams and visions may perhaps be methods of discernment or revelation from God.

While writing a book was the furthest thing from my mind; on February 25, 2019, God had other plans. I was merely trying to complete my Doctor of Ministry project, and then something happened, this book was born. It is an understatement to say I was stressed. I had less than half the number of pages completed for my project and the deadline was fast approaching. Out of know where, I sat there telling God perhaps, I just need to graduate next year because I cannot complete the writing. God truly has a sense of humor, because I clearly heard the Spirit of God say, "You have grace for 2019, you had better get to writing."

Afterwards, the Spirit said, "You know this is a book, right?" Of course, I nixed it off thinking sure, I simply want this project done so that I can graduate. I was thinking, I have writers block on this project and God, is talking about me writing a book. I did not see how it could happen. I do not know if the directness of what God said scared me or if God gave a special anointing for the work to be written. But I do know that I was able to complete the writing in just a matter of days.

As exciting as it was to write this book, the struggle was real. I say struggle in the sense that it seemed that whenever I thought I was building momentum, shortly thereafter, a curve ball was thrown, and it would be months before I could get to writing again.

As a pastor, I was trying to hear from God on ways of reimagining ministry because of COVID-19, and, yes, I was stressed, depressed and confused. The mounting pressure sent me to the emergency room on Sunday morning, June 14, 2020. I spent approximately eight hours in the emergency room and had an opportunity to minister to one of the nurses. Interestingly, I told her that I was writing a book about dreams and visions, which was something I normally do not mention. However, through the ministry moment, I heard the Spirit say to relax about the book. While I was waiting to have tests done, I had an unusual encounter with the Holy Spirit. I was communing with God and asking questions without opening my mouth and in my head, God was answering the questions that I posed. I was awe struck that I could hear God with such clarity that I had not previously experienced.

The thought of not completing an assignment from God lingered with me as I questioned whether the book would ever get written. Despite everything, I knew I heard the voice of God in 2019 and yet, in 2023, four years later, I had not published a book. I thought my season had passed, but God reassured me on April 25, 2023, at 7:16 am, God revealed to me via a dream that my daughter and I were going to write this book together. I saw the front of the book with both of our names on it. A lightbulb went off in my spirit and I immediately knew that I did not miss God. If I had rushed to get the book completed prior to April of 2023, I would have let an opportunity pass to co-author a book with my daughter.

A frequent saying of one of my friends is that "God does not waste any of life's experiences." With that said, prior to my salvation experience, while living in South Carolina, in the early 70's, I had dreams about numbers that ended up being dates that something special would occur. I often reflect on instances where I gave people numbers that I dreamed of, and they won money. Although I was involved in church activities such as singing in the choir and ushering, I cannot say that I had a personal relationship with the Lord Jesus. But I heard a voice say to me "don't do that anymore." I took that to mean, do not give anyone the numbers that I had received in dreams. In hindsight, I have a better understanding of the Scripture passage in Jeremiah 1:5 (NRSV) "Before I formed you in the womb, I knew you, and before you were born, I consecrated you; I appointed you to be a prophet to the nations," I have come to the realization that God was protecting what was already in me. Jeremiah is one of my favorite books and the passage reassures me that before I had surrendered my life to the Lord, the Holy Spirit had already determined what my gifts and journey experience would be. I was operating in the gifts of a word of wisdom and word of knowledge, but it was not being used to glorify God. I pray that if while reading this book and it speaks to you, that you too, will embrace what God is doing in you, then be grateful for God's grace and mercy as we continue to mature.

The Genesis of the Book

By Brandice Green Weathers, Ph.D.

There was a period in my life (late teens and early twenties) where I felt constantly unsettled. It was a nagging feeling that I couldn't quite remember something or that I had experienced something but couldn't quite remember the details. These experiences were occurring frequently, maybe several times a week and were starting to create a level of dread in my life. I don't recall when or how the Holy Spirit showed me that these experiences were actually me just remembering dreams, but with this clarification almost immediately the dread went away. At this point, I was very relieved to be free of the feeling of dread but then the question became what am I supposed to do with these dreams? I am embarrassed to say for a long time I just ignored them because I didn't understand the point or the purpose. The more I tried to ignore them the more I would dream.

In 1 Samuel 3, there is an interesting story about a little boy, Samuel, who while he is in bed hears someone calling his name and thinks it is his teacher, Eli, so he keeps getting out of bed and approaching Eli who keeps saying I am not calling you. After the third time, Eli understands that it is God calling Samuel, and he tells Samuel when he hears the voice next time to answer "Speak, LORD for your servant is listening." Once Samuel acknowledges God and demonstrates he is willing to listen, the conversation began, and God told Samuel about his vision (1 Samuel 3:11-15).

Finally, after years of me just trying to ignore the dreams and ultimately not being willing to participate in the conversation that God was trying to have with me, I finally asked God ...what are you trying to tell me with these dreams? This change in posture immediately changed everything and has provided me with the peace for which I was searching. When my mom approached me about contributing to this book, I eventually realized I was being given the opportunity to share how God has used dreams to grow my understanding about God and about myself. I hope that by sharing some of my dreams that you will see how God can reinforce what we know to be true from the Scriptures – that God is all-knowing, creative, loving, merciful, gracious, and so much more. So, reader, I pray that this book will inspire you to lean into your dreams and see them as a starting point and invitation to participate in a conversation with the creator of the universe. Be bold in your expectation to hear from God and to be included in His exciting vision.

Introduction

We are thrilled to be able to write this book as a mother and daughter duo. It is our desire to take you our readers on an extraordinary journey, delving deep into the realm of dreams and visions. Drawing from personal experiences and spiritual insights we will intertwine storytelling with profound wisdom, offering a unique perspective on how these encounters can illuminate the path to discovering the heart of God. In God's infinite wisdom, God has decided one of the ways to bring God's kingdom here on earth (as it is in heaven) is to partner with God image bearers (that's us). At a cursory glance, this seems risky since it is heavily dependent on the willingness of us to consistently listen and act on God's plan. What if I told you that God wanted to share God's vision and partner with you, God's friend). How God shares God's vision is God's prerogative but one of the ways God gives us glimpses into God's plan are through dreams and visions.

This is a non-fiction book written for Christians to whom God speaks to frequently through dreams and visions. The purpose for this writing is so that you understand that dreams and visions can be used as a tool of discernment. Dreams are defined as pictures, words, phrases, or images that one receives while asleep. A vision, likewise, either is a supernatural impartation delivered to a person in a dream or while one is awake. While the Bible does mention visions and dreams, the description of dreams and visions often overlaps.[1] Dreams and visions are useful tools of discernment within the faith-based community; however, one must be attentive in listening to what is revealed for discernment to take place. "Although dreams and visions are not listed as gifts in the Bible, they can and have been used as conduits through which the spiritual gifts flow."[2]

For example, for some, dreams and visions may operate with the spiritual gifts of the word of knowledge and word of wisdom. To discern God, it is essential to be in communion with God through a strong prayer life and the study of God's Word. It is crucial to understand that dreams and visions cannot replace the Word of God, nor can it replace our private quiet time of prayer and meditation. In the book "Discerning The Voice of God: How To Recognize When God Is Speaking," Priscilla

---

[1] John A. Sanford, Dreams God's Forgotten Language. (New York: J.B. Lippincott Company, 1968), 98.
[2] Jane Hamon, Dreams & Visions. (Minneapolis: Chosen, 2016), 108.

Shirer (92) stated, "Like Samuel, like Mary, like Saul—
God meets you where you are, God speaks in a way He
knows you can hear" (Shirer). Deuteronomy 29:29
(NRSV) speaks to this point: "The secret things belong to
the Lord our God, but the revealed things belong to us
and to our children forever, to observe all the words of
this law." It is being in the presence of the Lord that we
can discern what God's will is for our life. Now I want to
be clear that just because God reveals a thing to us, it
does not mean that God will reveal all the trials,
challenges, struggles nor blessings which we will
encounter. However, God discloses enough to
encourage us on the journey. In other words, think of it
as the DASH. There is a beginning and an ending date,
but we are not filled in on all the things which will occur
between.

Dreams and visions from God give us the honor
and privilege of seeing what is in the heart of God for a
person or thing and to hear what God wants to say about
the situation. It is important to demonstrate that you value
what God has given you by writing it down (or recording
them). Many times, without chronicling them the memory
of dreams will fade. The written account is not only
confirmation, but it will serve as encouragement during
the times when you question what you have seen. The

validation of your dreams will become invaluable as the enemy will try to convince you to doubt what God has told you. Are you willing to treat your dreams as the gift and opportunity that it is - the chance to partner with the Creator to bring God's will here on earth?

The book is organized into the following chapters:

Chapter 1 Salvation Preparation - I often wondered how much thought we give to the circumstances surrounding our salvation. Do we perhaps think of the people who casually or intentionally shared Christ with us or possibly said that they were praying for us. In the Gospel of John Chapter 4, Jesus by design, traveled through Samaria to get to Galilee. He stopped at a well at noon in Sychar because He needed to meet an unnamed woman. Jesus had a conversation with a Samaritan woman without a male presence at the well. His questions stimulated her curiosity and through His dialogue with her, she was convinced that He was the Messiah. The woman ran and told others in the town of her encounter with a man who told her everything that she ever did. This woman wanted others to experience what she felt. As she shared her story of her discovery of the Messiah many Samaritans believed in Him. God has unique ways for preparing our heart for salvation. This chapter will give insight into how the words of others and life circumstances, including 2-3 years of happiness, struggles, challenges, and a move that was life changing, were all part of God's salvation plan.

Chapter 2 Calling & Destiny - The Bible is filled with call stories of both men and women, from Abraham, Moses, Samuel, Jeremiah to Joseph and Junia. God calls whomever God desires, and because God is God, each call is unique. I have always been fascinated with the story of Joseph. Perhaps my interest in Joseph is because I am also a dreamer. Studying the story of Joseph provided me with great insight and I too learned from my mistakes as I was naive on exactly who and what to share what God reveals. Analyzing the story of Joseph helped me to better understand the calling that God has on my life and my destiny.

Chapter 3 Warnings - The Apostle Paul admonishes every believer to put on the whole armor of God daily since the enemy as a roaring lion is seeking whom he may destroy. Therefore, I am more convinced than ever that it is important for us to walk in the spirit each moment of the day to avoid the trappings of the devil. God warns us of pitfalls if only we take the time to listen to the what the Spirit is revealing.

Chapter 4 Directions and Guidance - God gives directions and guidance for decisions in which we are seeking an answer: although not in the traditional sense.

Chapter 5 Discernment – The Holy Spirit provides understanding on how dreams alert and reveal things which we would not otherwise know.

Chapter 6 Encouragement – Jeremiah 29:11 reminds us that God has always had a plan for us, even during times of discouragement, and sometimes God chooses to use dreams to reassure us of who is in control of our affairs.

Chapter 7 Prayers for the Church – As believers of Jesus, it is our responsibility to intercede on behalf of the body of Christ. As we would not know in the natural, however, through dreams and visions, God often reveals and nudges us to pray on behalf of the kingdom of God.

Chapter 8 Testimonies – Testimonials are important, as they encourage us to continue in the faith. A good reminder is the passage of Scripture in Revelation 12:11a (NIV) which states "they triumphed over him by the blood of the lamb and the word of their testimony." This Scripture provides insight as to the importance of testimonies and how they can be used to bless the body of Christ.

Chapter 9 Strategies for Interpreting Dreams - There is no better place to begin to explore strategies for interpretating dreams than asking the Holy Spirit for the interpretation and searching the Scripture to determine if what is revealed can be verified by the Word of God. Additionally, seeking the guidance of those who have a record of accurately interpreting dreams is also an approach to take.

Chapter 10 Journaling - "Write the vision; make it plain on tablets, so he may run who reads it. For still the vision awaits its appointed time; it hastens to the end—it will not lie. If it seems slow, wait for it; it will surely come; it will not delay" (Habakkuk 2:2-3). These words will serve as the foundation for a practice of journaling and why it is imperative not to ignore the warnings we receive.

Finally, it is our prayer that this book will encourage readers who have felt that what you are experiencing is not of God because you haven't heard much of dreams in the Christian arena. Let us reassure you God is speaking to more persons than we can fathom. God is making the connection, and it is our prayer that this book will help connect the dots.

Chapter 1

Salvation Preparation

In Acts 10:3-19, God was making salvation available to Cornelius, a Gentile. God dispatched an angel to inform Cornelius to contact Peter to travel to Joppa. While Peter was on the rooftop, he fell into a trance and had a vision from God revealing a sheet lowered to the ground by its four corners with all types of four-footed creatures and reptiles and birds of the air. A voice instructed Peter to "kill and eat" and further instructed him to go with the Gentile men who were at the door searching for him. God used the vision to instruct Peter to share the gospel message with a Gentile named Cornelius and his family. In Peter's vision, the sheet was symbolic that God was also making God's gift of salvation available to the Gentiles, those the Jews considered unclean.

In my early years as an employee of International Paper Company, I was having a challenging time with one of my managers. I can recall shortly after we purchased a home in June 1982, I had a conversation with one of my mangers, Raymond Jett Freeman, who was a Christian. I told Jett that we had just purchased a house and I needed to know if management was contemplating terminating my employment. I explained how I felt stressed because regardless of what I did in the department, a couple of the managers always seem to find fault with it. I knew Jett, however, was different, he was a Christian and would periodically talk to me about the Lord. I thought I was fine because I attended church, I was in the choir, and an usher. But there was a sense of calm and peace about him that drew me to him. He told me that he was praying for me. I can recall thinking there was something that I needed, but I did not know what it was.

During this time, my husband began receiving invitations for job interviews for various accounting jobs with International Paper Company. He interviewed for jobs in Baton Rouge, Louisiana, and Androscoggin, Maine. I desperately wanted to leave the harassment behind and urged him to take the job in Maine. Our daughter was about 2 years old, and my husband said while driving to the office in Maine, he drove over an hour before he saw any African Americans. He said we were not going to rear a family in a town where we would be the only Black family. Since my husband was interviewing for jobs, I was thinking that I was restless because I wanted to move. Little did I know that the restlessness was because my soul was yearning for more than I was receiving. It was yearning for a relationship with the Lord Jesus Christ.

My husband was offered a position at International Paper's headquarters in Manhattan, New York and he accepted. We were excited about the move and went house hunting in early fall. My husband was going to leave before us, and our daughter and I would join him later. We left South Carolina in October 1983 and were on interim living until the end of December. We moved into the new home we purchased in Flanders, New Jersey on December 31. It was one of the coldest days I had ever experienced. It took several days for the house to warm up because the doors were constantly open as the furniture was being moved into the house.

My husband had been researching African Methodist Episcopal (AME) churches while he was in New Jersey and shortly after our daughter and I arrived, we began visiting Bethel AME Church in Boonton, New Jersey. The church was not on the beaten path. The white structure sat at the top of the hill. It was in the middle of an affluent city, Mountain Lakes, New Jersey. It was certainly divinely orchestrated since not many AME's knew there was an AME Church in Boonton, New Jersey.

Our daughter fell in love with the church. The Pastor, the Reverend James E. Deas, Sr., was a Bible teaching, anointed man who believed in the gifts of the Spirit, laying on of hands, speaking in tongues, etc. The first Sunday we attended, we sat on the last pew in the church. We sat at the back of the church for two reasons. One of course is obvious, we were new. Secondly, I noticed Reverend Deas laying hands on individuals, and they would fall. I, on the other hand, did not have a personal relationship with the Lord, Jesus and I had never experienced anyone laying hands on anyone and seeing them slain in the Spirit. And certainly, I never heard anyone speaking in tongues and the interpretation being given. I thought to myself, what have we gotten ourselves into? I was surprised but should not have been, Reverend Deas discerned that I was uncomfortable with what I was observing. Therefore, he gave me a document explaining what we had experienced.

I was ready to leave, but our daughter who was 3½ years old, said this church is just like Granddaddy Green's church, so we remained. To this day, I am still perplexed about that because to me there was nothing at the church in New Jersey that reminded me of the church my father-in-law attended.

Then, each Sunday we moved up one pew until I finally rested on the third pew. We attended Sunday School each week and our daughter became involved in the children's choir. On Sunday, March 4, 1984, it seemed as if I was catapulted to the altar, and I was on my knees. The only thing that I remembered was that I was in the Spirit and when I woke up, I was speaking in tongues, and then I remembered the dream from the previous night. On Saturday, March 3, 1984, I had a dream of a woman wearing a cream blouse and a black/white checkered skirt with pockets kneeling at the altar. I can recall that in the dream, I was attempting to see the face of the person at the altar, but no matter which angle I attempted to see the person, I could not see the face. In the dream I was wearing the outfit that I wore to church the next day. Hindsight is 20/20 because although I was dreaming, God did not allow me to discern that I was seeing myself.

Following my conversion, I understood that the prayers of Jett and others softened my heart to surrender to the Lord Jesus. God wanted me to know that the move was designed for me had to do with more than a place but about my salvation and relationship with the Lord Jesus. There have been countless times that I have reminisced and amazed on how we landed at Bethel AME in Boonton, New Jersey.

God was growing me in ways that I did not understand. I began spending hours studying the Word and then I felt the urge to pray without prompting. It was during this time that I began to understand the gifts of the Spirit. Mrs. Ruth Deas, wife of Pastor Deas purchased a book for me entitled "The Holy Spirit And His Gifts," it was a red 8 ½ x 11 size-book by Kenneth E. Hagin. The book gave examples of the various gifts and how it operated. Years later, I was prophesied that two of the gifts that I had received were the gift of the word of knowledge and the gift of the word of wisdom. I have since come into the realization that the gifts of the word of knowledge and wisdom are in operation through dreams and visions as a means of the prophetic intercessory prayer ministry that God was calling me to embark upon.

I cannot say that I recall having dreams prior to my late teens. I began journaling sometime in the late eighty's but was not consistent with it because of the number of dreams I would have per night and the length of time that it took to record. I have asked God to forgive me for my ignorance and lack of understanding for not valuing what had been given me. For years in the 1980's - 2015 I was not consistent with journaling. I was immature and not fully understanding the big picture of the dreams. Some dreams, although not recorded with dates or times, are etched in my memory forever. Therefore, what is recorded in the pages of this book are intimate details of dreams that have impacted my life and the lives of others. The dreams have helped me to make decisions as I prayed for the interpretation. It was the Reverend Shirley Owens Prince who allowed me to share openly in the area of dreams and visions, and she spoke to me about the gifts, which helped me to understand that the dreams were God's way to direct me how to pray and that what I had was a gift and not to take it lightly.

Chapter 2

Calling & Destiny

It is fascinating for me to read of the various call stories in the Bible. But I must admit the one that intrigues me the most is the call of Samuel found in 1 Samuel 3:2-21. Perhaps the reason for my fascination is the conversation and nurturing that took place between Samuel and his mother, Hannah. I am imagining how she must have given testimony of how he was prayed into being and how she vowed he would be devoted to the Lord prior to his birth. This would have been a major step in his faith journey to become obedient to God as a youth receiving a Word from God rebuking, Eli, the priest, and the one who had mentored him and whom he served in ministry. This story is a reminder of the obligation to walk worthy of our calling. Perhaps Samuel recalled how his mother had said he was to dedicate himself to the service of the Lord forever.

In addition to God speaking to me through dreams and visions, a part of my calling, the Holy Spirit has graciously endowed me with is the ability to intercede on behalf of others. While my dream often includes family members and clergy persons however, my assignment from God is to pray for specific leaders in the United States. Although my dreams are focused on leaders in the United States, I do pray for world leaders.

My call to the ministry came in 1984 in a dream, I saw Jesus standing in the vestibule, holding a blue Bible, which was unusual because it had Jesus' picture on the front and back. He walked me from the vestibule to the pulpit and stood me behind the podium and said, "Teach My Word and preach My Word."

The call to teach the Bible confirmed the dream "Teach My Word." We relocated to Memphis in the summer of 1987. We visited several AME Churches in Memphis, but we finally settled on St. James AME after hearing Reverend Prince preach at one of the AME churches we visited. It was during the fall of 1987 that Brandi and I began going to the Bible Study each Saturday which was taught by Reverend Prince. Shortly after, we began attending Bible Study, Reverend Prince and her family adopted my family. We were invited to holiday celebrations and cookouts and Brandi soon adopted Mrs. Lavina Owens, Reverend Prince's mother, as her grandmother. Mrs. Owens attended the grandmother's functions at Brandi's school and would take Brandi home with her after the functions. Little did I know that God was orchestrating the events of my life.

During the spring of 1988, Reverend Prince asked me to teach a few of the Bible Study sessions, which I did. After preparing for several weeks, I said to myself, "This is okay for Reverend Prince, but this is too much work for me." While attending a Memorial Day cookout at Mrs. Owens' home, Reverend Prince was quizzing me on the assignments, and I was saying to myself that I could put up with it for a couple more weeks.

I can recall so vividly that we traveled to South Carolina to my parents' home for the Christmas holiday in December 1988. The very first night that we arrived, God gave me a dream, but this dream was unusual because I did not see Reverend Prince, but saw the disciple, Peter, and I heard the voice that said, "Shirley is waiting on you Barbara and do not lean on Peter but lean on Jesus." I sat straight up in the bed and said, "Why would Shirley be waiting on me when we just arrived in South Carolina?" I had misinterpreted the dream and did not understand that what God was saying to me, was not to become dependent on Reverend Prince, but to lean on Jesus. Furthermore, I learned that Reverend Prince was going to be leaving the AME Church and would unite with Mississippi Boulevard Christian Church, but she could not leave until she had someone to teach the Bible Study at St. James. I began teaching the Bible Study at St. James in 1989 and taught it until 1999. Hence, the dream that God had given me back in 1984 that I would teach God's Word and then preach God's Word was slowly being fulfilled.

Dreams have been treated as irrelevant by many, and, largely marginalized as a discernment tool in community. Therefore, persons like Jarena Lee, the first female licensed to preach in the AME Church in 1819, wrote about her own experience, as a testimony to the value of dreams. It took Lee eight years to respond to the dream in which she received her call to preach (cited in Preaching as Testimony by Anna Carter Florence). The delay was not a matter of uncertainty. Her dreams revealed God's will for her life, "Lee doubted her own message." Finally, her health caught her attention. She had an episode where she became physically and spiritually sick. Lee determined that the dream was of God, and she acted upon the revelation in the dream. She did not take the role of dreams seriously, nor did her community. What would have happened if Lee had been encouraged to consider her dream as part of her call to ministry?

Akin to what Lee experienced, my surrender came almost seven years after experiencing a constant headache that would not subside unless I read the Word of God, hence, I realized that God was indeed calling me into the ministry; however, the enemy did not want me to accept the call. Finally, after much struggle, I answered my call in October 1990 my headaches went away immediately, in November 1990, I received my license to preach, and my pastoral ministry began in 1996.

Unlike Jarena Lee who had no mentor who suggested that dreams could be useful in discernment, I did have individuals who I trusted and could at least share my dreams. Without a doubt, the Bible confirms that God wants to and does communicate with God's people and that God uses various methods in which to do so. We on the other hand, must cooperate and be available and open to God. There are numerous instances in Scripture of dreams and visions, yet published Christian literature is almost nonexistent to teach and train individuals on understanding and interpreting dreams and visions and their importance to the Christian faith.

Biblically, recorded dreams and visions were employed as a means of God speaking to God's people to direct, motivate, enlighten, encourage, and warn the people. Today, there is still a need for those in leadership in the Church who dream dreams and see visions to operate in them, explain how they operate in integrity within the body of Christ, and stress the importance to the faith community.

The story of Joseph and his dreams, visions and interpretation as revealed in Scripture provides insight that God was directing Joseph at an early age and uncovering his purpose in life. Joseph's first dream brought to light that his brothers' sheaves bowed down to his and a second dream made known that the sun, moon and the eleven stars bowed to Joseph (Genesis 37:5-10). The dreams which God revealed to Joseph contained symbols; hence, the interpretation of the dreams was unknown by Joseph. Although Joseph was probably unclear on the exact meaning of the dream, his father pondered the probable interpretation in his heart.

God provided Joseph the interpretation of two separate dreams of Pharaoh which were the same. The king dreamed of seven plump ears eaten up by the seven thin ears. Again, he dreamed and this time, seven fat cows were eaten by seven thin, ugly cows and the thin cows' appearance did not change after eating the fat cows. Joseph was able to discern that God was informing the king that there would be seven years of abundant crops in the land and seven years of famine. Hence, because of Joseph's wisdom, he was given a strategy to store goods during the seven years of abundance to combat the years of scarcity which was to come. An entire nation was saved from famine and benefited as a result of Joseph's gifts. Although Joseph was immature in the use of his gifts, ultimately what he saw materialized although the struggles and trials he would encounter prior to his brothers bowing down to him were not revealed to him by God (Genesis 41:15-32, 53-54). The revelation that came from God in a dream to Joseph concerning him, his family, and a nation, was realized when Joseph's brothers came to Egypt because of the famine in the land.

Likewise, we are living in difficult times and individuals are seeking answers; therefore, as God discloses information to us through dreams and visions, we should be channels through which the destiny of others may be realized because of our obedience to share what God revealed.

As a person who has several dreams per night, upon awakening, I am trying to determine not only what the dream means, but what God desires for me to do with what I saw.

51

Dr. Barbara Holmes, President Emerita of United Theological Seminary of the Twin Cities and writer, noted a way in which dreams impact the course of a person's life. She stated that Carl G. Jung coined the phrase "big dream" in reference to personal dreams that are so significant that the impact experienced by a person is for a lifetime."[3] I concur with Jung, as I have had dreams from more than thirty years ago that I did not record (recording would have allowed me to see what season I was in and help me to know that I received the dream from God); however, the details of the dreams are as fresh today as the day when they were given to me.

Even as I advocate alongside other leaders for the use of dreams for discernment, I believe it is important to stress that the Word of God and the Holy Spirit are the lenses through which we filter dreams. Therefore, it is unwise to think that God will direct our every movement by dreams and visions. Any dream or vision revealed by God will always align with Scripture.

The fall of 1984; I experienced my second time seeing Jesus in a dream. I do not recall what was happening in my life at the time. Jesus was wearing all white, He seemed to shine so brightly. When I saw

[3] Barbara A. Holmes, Dreaming. (Minneapolis: Fortress Press, 2012), 8.

Jesus, I fell at His feet, and said, "He is beautiful." What was strange to me in the dream is that Jesus seemed to place what looked like a pen or some object over my eyes and when I got up, I was strengthened.

I had several dreams on Monday, November 8, 2004, however, in this dream, I was blessed to have the vision of Jesus. This was the third time that I had seen Jesus in a dream. In this dream, God showed me that I was talking to Jesus. I saw that I was wearing my black robe, but it was ripped on the left side, and pinned. I put my white robe over it, and I was crying. I told Jesus to tell God that I was sorry, but this is so hard. I said that I was sorry that I did not do what God expected. I was surprised, but Jesus' response was, "You are one of the few persons who takes Me for who I am." I honestly believe that the God allowed me to see Jesus during my dream, because it was a difficult season that seemed to last for years.

When God calls us into ministry, God also gives a glimpse concerning not only the blessings, but provides warnings sometimes through dreams with symbols, if we are attentive, we might see more insight into some of the challenges we will face as we journey through life. For example, on November 11, 2004, God allowed me to see individuals staring at my direction, but they were asking each other where I was. What was interesting was that I was right in front of them, but they could not see me. Then the scenery changed, and I was in Africa along with some other individual that I knew. A preacher that I knew well was angry and inquired how I was able to travel to Africa. Then I, along with the other person who was with me, hid in a jungle area. We eventually left where we were hiding and arrived at this beautiful white building and the person who was with me told me that I was safe. I started to go outside looking for something but could not remember what it was that I was searching for, but I looked outside and saw a dark dirt road and decided not to leave, but to remain where I was.

The scenery changed and I saw several female preachers in a pulpit and there was a small pillow. One of the preachers wanted to give the pillow to me, but I said that the pillow was for the bishop, and that I would give the pillow to the bishop. We all knelt to pray. I began praying that God would bless all those who were present. Somehow, I overheard the other people were praying, and I realized that I was asking God to do something for others while the other preachers were thanking and praising God.

Then my mentor, Reverend Shirley Owens Prince, appeared in the dream and asked me if I knew why I was going through what I was going through and I responded by saying "Sorta, kinda." Then I responded that God is attempting to take me to another level in Him. The dream also taught me that in addition to petitioning God on behalf of others, I should be praising and thanking God. It is a constant reminder when I begin to pray to always give God praise and adoration for who God is, what God has done, is doing and for what has not yet been manifested.

On May 15, 2013, I received an email from a former co-worker, Lori Dixon. She stated that in 2001 or 2002 (10 or 11 years earlier), I had approached her about a dream that God had given me telling her that she was going to enter the ministry. Lori stated that I said she was standing on stage speaking to a large group and the room was packed. Some of the names of the people who were in the audience worked with us at International Paper. I did not share that I saw her standing at a pulpit because I did not want to alarm her since I was able to discern that she was not ready to accept that she was called into the ministry. Lori acknowledged that she was not ready to accept that word from God. But on March

31, 2013, she acknowledged her call into the preaching ministry. Lori thanked me for sharing what God had given me earlier for her. She stated that her pastor asked her how she knew she had been called, she shared that someone had prophesied to her eleven years earlier and that the dream I gave her was one of her spiritual markers establishing her call. She also shared that I had impacted her life.

The timing of this confirmation was especially important to me in a season of personal trauma. Our first and only granddaughter had died suddenly on April 2, 2013. I was doubting and struggling on whether I was hearing from God through dreams and visions. I was wondering how and why God could reveal to me information about others and only provided a date which ending up being the date that our granddaughter died.

I had to come to terms with what I wanted to know versus my need to know and totally trust a loving God. I have reconciled that although one may have spiritual gifts and insight, it is God who chooses what and how much to reveal.

When I came into the knowledge of Christ, I was encouraged by my Pastor to believe that the spiritual gifts of the word of wisdom and word of knowledge were in operation through the dreams and visions I was receiving from God. However, upon relocating from the Northeast and under the leadership of several pastors, I noticed that dreams and visions had not been endorsed as a means by which God speaks to believers in the southern United States. In Morton Kelsey's book *Dreams: A Way to Listen to God,* (15) he states, and I concur, that "the church today faces numerous problems because it is no longer grounded in spiritual reality; therefore, the church is unable to connect and address the issues that plague the lives of God's people." It was not uncommon for God to disclose the revelation of dreams and visions to individuals in the Old Testament such as Daniel, Joseph, Abraham, and Solomon. Likewise, biblical characters such as Joseph, husband of Mary, and the Apostle Paul in the New Testaments are among those to have dreams and visions.

Chapter 3

Warnings

Dreams can reveal guiding lights for those who listen, but they can also share news of danger. The Scriptures are full of examples of prophets giving warning to those who are in positions of leadership. One such instance is found in 2 Kings 6:8-12. The king of Syria was at war with Israel. The king would draw up his plan on where he would mobilize his troops. Each time the king drew up his battle plans, God would give the prophet Elisha the information, and the prophet would notify the king of Israel to stay away from the location which would become a trap for Israel. The king of Israel would send a scout to research the matter to determine if the information he had received from the prophet was accurate. God provided this information several times. This revelation frustrated the king of Syria so much that he corralled his officers to determine who the traitor was among the ranks. Then one of the officers of the king of Syria spoke up, and to the king of Syria's surprise he was informed that not only does the prophet Elisha inform the king of Israel of his battle plans, but the things that are spoken in the privacy of your bedroom are also revealed to the prophet.

Likewise, throughout my life and ministry, the Lord has revealed to me through dreams things that I needed to have my spiritual antenna receive. For example, on November 21, 1994, I dreamed that I got out of bed and went into my study to read my Bible. When I got there my dog, Sissy, was standing in the middle of the bed afraid to get down. I told her to get down and I tried to run her downstairs. But when I got to the stairs, I saw that a vacuum cleaner was on about the third step from the bottom. When I looked, I observed that my front door was open, and I was thinking why my husband, Arch, left the front door open like that. Then I saw 4 persons a man in the back and 3 women, one brown-skinned that was trying to come toward me. I screamed to the top of my voice, then I started raising my hand and singing in the name of Jesus. I ran upstairs and told Brandi to close her door and she did. Arch was asleep and I tried to wake him, but I couldn't. I then started to run into the bathroom and call someone to help. At that moment a voice said that I had better use what I had. I jumped in the bed and then I woke up. I went back to sleep and entered the same dream. This time the people turned into snakes and Arch was still sleeping. I noticed a black snake that seemed to stretch from my front door to my bed. I grabbed the snake by the neck and held on to it and said in the Name of Jesus and it wiggled out of my hand and burst through the front door. I ran downstairs and saw 2 ladies and a child; the ladies were wearing red dresses and they asked what that was. I responded by saying that I cast that devil out of my house and that I was going to use the authority God has given me in the Name of Jesus and I said that the devil cannot stay here. One of those ladies said whatever it was, it came down the stairs vomiting as it went out. Then a ray of sunlight engulfed my home.

The interpretation that came was that there was an invasion in my home, the vacuum cleaner represents removing dirt or things that should not be there. The people who later turned into snakes represent the enemy. The dream was letting me know that there is power in the name of Jesus and that I needed to take the authority and use the name.

Another example of a warning came in a dream on June 28, 1995, there were 4 persons in leadership who were relaxing around a table and discussing how they were going to keep me back. In the dream I confronted the persons and said to them God has allowed me to see what you are doing, and I described the scenery and called them "low down preachers." Then the scenery changed and there was a storm all around my house with wind blowing but not the disturbance around anyone else's home in the community. I went and put on my raincoat and hat so that I could walk in the rain. The wind and rain were blowing so hard that it almost blew the patio furniture, which I do not own, away. I turned and saw my husband standing there and a preacher that we know placed his hand on my husband's shoulder and told him that everything was going to be alright. I was not in pastoral ministry, but the season in my ministry was challenging.

At various times, God disclosed to me tactics of the enemy through dreams during difficult times in my life and ministry. I can recall during one of my pastoral assignments that God divulged that rockets were being fired at me. The rockets, however, would not hit me because there were individuals on top of me covering me to prevent the rocket from getting to me. One month from the date of the dream, it was manifested in the natural what the dream was concerning. There were individuals whom God has sent to speak on my behalf. God is our guide and as we are instructed in Proverbs 3:5-6, we are not to lean to our own understanding but in all our ways acknowledge God and God will direct our paths.

Regardless of how insignificant you may think a dream is, it is wise to pay attention to it and the details within. The objects in the dream may be symbolic and not literal. For example, on September 17, 2003, in a dream God showed me what appeared to be a pool house, but it was black. Then the scenery changed, and I recalled that there was a roll of paper towel near the stove. When I looked closer, I saw the fire and the pool house exploded, or I guess I should say burned because I did not hear an explosion. On September 24, 2003, which is one week later, I placed a sweet potato in the microwave on a setting which was too high, and the paper towel and the sweet potato burned. As I interpreted the dream afterward God was trying to warn me that the I was going to cook the sweet potato on a setting that was too high, and it could cause a fire. However, I did not pay close enough attention to the dream or I would have been able to discern that placing the sweet potato in the microwave on a setting too high for it, is a potential fire risk. Again, I stress that items in a dream can be literal or symbolic as was seen in the dream I quoted. The small black pool house was my microwave oven.

Similar to my mom, I don't remember the first time God gave me a dream, but I do recall when someone recognized that I was a dreamer. I was at a youth revival and when it was my time to be anointed and prayed for by Reverend Peal Lurry, she said, "Oh this baby has dreams." I remember being shocked that someone knew that about me.

Again, like mom, in August 2007, I had just finished an important proposal for graduate school. I was so excited because it was a big step on the way to completing my Ph.D. degree. A night or two after my proposal, I dreamed that fiery darts were being shot at me, but I was under an invisible dome that was protecting me. There were flames everywhere around me, but I was untouched because the arrows were being blocked by the dome.

The next afternoon there was a fire caused by a grill on a deck that was in my apartment building. When the fire started, I heard yells of people warning others to get out of the building. I grabbed my backpack (with laptop), keys, and put on my flip flops. I ran outside and looked at the fire. My car was at the front of the building. The police had already arrived and were starting to block access to the front of the building, but I asked if I could move my car. Thankfully, they allowed me to move my car minutes before the fire fighters came. I went to a church member's house figuring we would be back in the building later that night. Well, that night, they were still fighting the fire, it was like nothing I had ever seen. By the end of it, the building had collapsed on itself and the only things that I had were the clothes I had on, my laptop, and my car. I believe that dream was a warning of the impending trouble to come, and the dome was a reminder that I was protected by the Holy Spirit. When I think of this dream, it always reminds me of the assurance of Psalm 91 (NIV).

2 "He is my refuge and my fortress,
my God, in whom I trust."

...

4He will cover you with his feathers,
and under his wings you will find refuge;
his faithfulness will be your shield and rampart.
5 You will not fear the terror of night,
nor the arrow that flies by day"

Although this was a very stressful time in my life, I had no apartment, I lost almost all my things, and I was still in school. Through it all God was with me and protecting me just like His Word says and how the dream showed me. The love of God was revealed in so many ways. My church family provided me so much support. Friends from church allowed me to stay with them until I found another apartment, which took about a month. Other members prayed for me and checked in on me. I had renter's insurance and was able to replace everything that was lost in the fire (furniture, electronics, clothing, etc.). While I waited for the insurance process, church members were so loving and sent me money, bed linens, cookware, and other things that I would need for my new place.

In the end I found out with God, I was able to withstand more than I ever thought. Despite all the chaos, I was enabled by God to complete my doctorate in Material Science and Engineering in December 2008. At that time, I wasn't sure how up to date my laptop was in comparison to my desktop. A week or so later my upstairs neighbor contacted and told me he found my computer tower under all the rubble of the apartment collapse. Although I had grabbed my laptop, when I ran out of my apartment not all my files were completely up to date. I thanked my neighbor and put the tower, which was covered with soot and ashes, in my car. Later, I tried it out, and the tower booted right up. I was able to access ALL my latest files. In the end I found out with God, I was able to withstand more than I ever thought. Despite all the chaos, I was enabled by God to complete my doctorate in December 2008.

I have come to the realization over the past year that everything has an expiration date. Regardless of how long and challenging the season may seem, God has a timetable for it, as stated in Ecclesiastes 3.

I have marveled on how God speaks to my daughter and me. Like the dream that Brandice (Brandi) had warning her about her apartment in 2007, God likewise warned me about an event.

In September 2015, my husband purchased me a Surface computer, with Microsoft full suite for our 37th wedding Anniversary. I was so excited, I took it everywhere and since it had the full Microsoft suite, it was as if I had a desktop computer in a purse. When I flew, I no longer had to struggle with a huge laptop bag. What I loved about the Surface was that it was small enough to fit in my purse or tote. I bought a turquoise case and a bright blue detachable keyboard with a stylus which made it even more convenient.

On January 2, 2016, at 12:47 am, I was awakened because of a new dream. This was the first dream that I had on January 2. I was at home when God revealed to me in the dream that I was crying because my Surface computer had been destroyed. It seemed as if I left my computer in a suitcase at a store or some place and somehow it was run over by a vehicle. The only thing that was left was the frame of the suitcase. In the dream, I kept repeating that everything that I had was on the computer and I did not have a backup. I kept a close eye on my computer and thought several times about purchasing an external hard drive, but never followed through on it.

When I woke up, I was saying it was only a dream. I thought it is a warning to keep a watch on my Surface while at the Evangelistic Conference that is hosted each year by Reverend Dr. James Carter Wade, director of the AME Department of Church Growth and Development.

On Tuesday, March 22, 2016, I was preparing to work on my computer. When I attempted to turn it on nothing happened except a black screen. I tried to shut it down by hitting the Ctrl and Alt keys and the Del button, but nothing happened. I decided to unplug and try to let the battery run down and recharge. I was unable to shut the computer off. I telephoned Microsoft and their resolution was to reset the computer to the factory setting. I was not going to try that because it meant that it would erase everything that I had on the computer, and I contacted one of my members who took the Surface to her job and a co-worker and friend charged it and on April 7, 2016, My Surface was restored. I was overjoyed and on April 8, 2016, I purchased an external hard drive and I have been faithful in backing up my computer at least once a week and if I am working on important documents, I will send the latest copy of the document(s) to my email and copy to the backup drive each night.

God is revealing, but are we seeing? In June 2019, I began preparing for my first "Seeing the Heart of God Through Dreams and Visions – I Have A Dream" Conference which was to be held September 27 and 28 in Memphis. My desire was to have an awesome move of God that would be experienced by everyone. In preparation for the time, a core group of intercessory prayer warriors and I had been in an intentional period of consecration with fasting and praying before the Lord. We were covering the participants, venue and every detail associated with the conference. Hence, I had numerous individuals contacting me about the conference, and I had numerous *to do* notes with contact information saved in the note section of my Samsung Galaxy 9 cellphone.

To say that I was exhausted from the preparation is an understatement. The week of September 2 was hectic. I had two dreams at 12:50 am on September 2. In the dream God revealed that my mother gave me a loaf of bread and two slices of bread. I received the loaf and the two single slices and held them close to my chest before I placed them on the top shelf. Then I noticed there were two women who were across the street looking and wondering why my mother was giving me bread. I sensed in the dream that they were concocting a scheme to take the bread. Half asleep, I jotted the dream down on a half piece of paper when I went to the bathroom.

Because of the hustle and bustle preparing for the conference, when I awakened, on Monday, I only recorded the second dream. That was a deviation from my normal schedule of recording my dreams each morning. On Tuesday, I scurried around preparing for Noon Bible Study at church, and again I failed to record the dream or give any thought to it. By the next morning when I woke up at 6:00 am, I was more concerned with trying to do a quick devotion and tackling my *to do* list than recording my dream. The day was filled with errands. I made what I thought was going to be a quick run to Walmart to get journals to give as door prizes at the conference. I also bought gifts for the presenters and some items for my grandnieces and nephew for school. It was approximately 4:30 pm as I was walking to the journal section, that I noticed a missed call from a clergy friend. And that's when I did something that I do not normally do – I talked on my cellphone as I shopped. I completed the call and without thinking, I placed my cellphone on the shelf while I looked at envelopes. A few minutes later, I went two aisles down and that's when it hit me: did I place my cell phone back in my purse? I hadn't. I was frantic and backtracked; my cellphone was not in my purse and nowhere to be found. I began praying, "*Lord Jesus, I cannot lose my phone, all of the contacts for this conference and the pictures of my grandbabies are in my phone.*" An employee noticed that I was frantic. She asked if she could help. I responded that I misplaced my phone and asked to use hers to make a call. Obviously, because I was panicky, I could only recall the mobile number for my husband and my armorbearer. Honestly, I did not want to contact my

71

husband because he had mentioned earlier during the day that I was doing too much and needed to slow down.

I dreaded having to tell him that I had lost my phone. I dialed my armorbearer. She did not recognize the number and did not pick up. I ran to the customer service counter to see if someone had turned in the phone. I was devastated. No one had turned it in. I was almost in tears and thought, "*I need to go to Verizon*," but I heard the Spirit of God say, "P*urchase those items for the children then go to Verizon.*" At the checkout, another employee was kind enough to allow me to use her cellphone. I attempted to contact my armorbearer again, and this time she picked up. I explained what happened and asked her to pray. I told her I was going to Verizon to try and trace the phone. I paid for the items, and off I went to Verizon.

When I arrived, I saw the representative who sold me the phone. I explained what happened. I was so discombobulated and could not recall my email password; without it, we could not track the phone. My armorbearer contacted the last person I spoke with prior to losing my phone and they began praying that whoever took the phone would not be able to hold it in their hands. She dialed my phone and the person who had taken the phone answered. My armorbearer asked, "*What are you doing with Pastor Green's phone and why did you not leave the phone at the customer service desk?*" The person said she would not speak with anyone except to the owner of the phone. My armorbearer responded that I was at Verizon, and the person with my phone said for me to meet her at a particular location and gave us the color of vehicle she was driving.

In the meantime, my armorbearer said she and her niece would meet me at home. She had alerted my husband about what was happening. When I got home, he asked, "*Where is your phone?*" I had to admit I had put it down and someone took it. He was upset when I told him that my armorbearer was coming to pick me up and we were going to meet the person. My husband decided to ride in a separate vehicle and follow us because he said it was dangerous what we were doing. When we arrived at the location, I dialed my phone. The person had lied to us about the color of the vehicle she was driving. We parked, got out, and realized we were parked next to a SUV where two women exited. The person in the passenger seat held my phone out as to say *I do not want to hold this phone.* I thanked them for returning the phone, told them that I was a pastor and had hundreds of contacts that I desperately needed. I asked why they did not leave the phone at the customer service desk? They gave me a lame excuse that someone had given the phone to them.

Sometimes dreams are treated as irrelevant, but in this instance, it was a warning. Wednesday was a long day, but at 6:54 pm, by the grace of God, I was in possession of my phone. The bread was symbolic of the phone of sustainability because I am helped and supported by it. The two slices of bread, which were out of place, were the two women, who looked just as God gave them to me in the dream. On my way home, I prayed that if this was the first time these individuals had stolen something, or if they had done it before, that it would be their last time.

Chapter 4

Directions & Guidance

It was mid-April 1987, when my husband, daughter, and I were house hunting, as we were relocating from the Northeast to Memphis, TN, in May. We had viewed between 30-40 homes and had a price range for the home we wanted to purchase. We wanted to live in Memphis and not in Germantown, where it seemed that most of the realtors were trying to steer homebuyers. After almost a week of viewing homes, we had almost given up and frankly I was beginning to panic since we would be moving to Memphis within a month, and we still had not found a house. None of the homes we had viewed were what my husband and I could agree to pay for a home. There was one house that I fell in love with and wanted, but my husband said there must be a reason why the house has been on the market for 9 months and not sold.

I knew God was aware how frustrated I was becoming. Therefore, I prayed that God would reveal to us the home that we were to purchase. I had a dream a night in April 1987, and God gave me a dollar amount of what we would purchase our home. I was excited;

however, all the homes that we had viewed cost much more than what I dreamed. I began to think, "are the prices of the home coming down to that amount and how would we know if the price was reduced overnight. God had other ideas. As we were to meet the realtor to view a few more homes, the realtor phoned and said she had information about a home that was going on the market later that day and wanted to know if we wanted to view it. We said sure and came to the house, it did not even have a for sale sign in the yard yet. As we walked in the house, my husband and I both said, "it feels like home."

As we walked through the home the draperies and color scheme matched everything that we had in our home in New Jersey. As we walked in the backyard, I heard the Spirit of God say, "Ask her (the realtor) how much do you think they would accept for the house?" The quote that the realtor gave me was the amount that the Lord had revealed in the dream. I mentioned that amount to my husband and said we should place an offer on the house.

We closed on the house on Tuesday, June 2, 1987, and it was interesting that when we met the couple at the closing, we found that the wife and I had the same first name. The couple was really nice, they brought the two garage openers and said that the window dressings would remain. The dream came true! We moved into the house on June 6, 1987, my birthday, and this house has been our home for 37 years.

God reminds us in Proverbs 3:5-6 that if we were to trust totally in the Lord with our entire being and not rely on our human understanding that God would direct our paths and give the guidance that is needed. As a preacher and Pastor, I am constantly seeking God for direction and guidance on how to lead the congregation and preach what God desires the Word to be for the people each time that I stand to proclaim it. Hence, on January 30, 2004, God revealed in a dream that my husband gave me a piece of paper with a couple of simple words. First, the words Aquila and Pricilla were written on it. Secondly, the word "capital" was written on it. I perceived that God was instructing me to preach from Acts 18:1-11 and one of the points was that capital, money is required to do ministry.

Additionally, God is concerned about everything that concerns us. I believe that God provides us with advance knowledge of what is to occur so that we can know that it is God. During the week of December 21, 2008, God gave me a dream that my position with the

77

company I had worked for 34 years was being eliminated. In the dream I saw a conference room and a mahogany table. When I woke up, I asked God if my job was being eliminated, but I did not receive an answer. In January 2009, my manager contacted me to conduct my yearly evaluation. We scheduled the meeting to be at the main office building since he was scheduled to be at that location for several meetings. I did not think it was an unusual request since he frequently attended meetings at that location. I can recall that it was a Friday, I arrived on the second floor and went to the conference room, since that is where the meeting was to occur. As soon as I arrived at the door of the conference room and saw the mahogany table and saw the Human Resources manager, I knew what God had revealed to me in December was going to come to pass. I experienced various emotions. For a few minutes, several emotions filled my very being. I was angry since I had given 34+ years of service to one company and to receive notice that I was being terminated felt unjust. I was scared because I would be 52 years of age before I was terminated. I wondered if I would be able to find another job at my salary or higher. Next, anger ensued and filled my very being. Once I prayed and asked God to calm me, I realized that things were going to work out for my good. God had given me a dream that my position was being terminated, so surely God had a plan for me. The severance package that was offered was mouth dropping. The package that was offered to those of us who were terminated in 2009 was not offered to another group. Additionally, I was given 6 months' notice before I would leave.

Moreover, I was informed by my manager that there were other positions that I qualified for within the company and that I could apply, and he would write a recommendation for me if I wanted to go that route. My co-workers came and talked to me once they learned of my situation. The first thing they said was we are praying for a position to become available. It became apparent that I had settled in my spirit that God was leading me because my response to my co-workers were "If God gave me a heads up about my position being eliminated, then it meant that God has something better for me."

My husband was already retired at this time, and when I came home and told him that my job had been eliminated. He was calm and said something about the fact that we were going to be fine financially. He mentioned the house was practically paid for and that was the only bill we had and the only reason we had not paid it off was because of the tax break. Additionally, he said that we were able to move funds and handle any unforeseen expense if needed. Normally, I would clean the house and do the laundry after work, but the direction of God, confirmed by my husband, felt pressing, I immediately set to work in the financial tasks. God had given me a sense of peace, and everything really was working out for my good. God was guiding my every step.

There were several things that occurred to confirm that God did have a plan and purpose for my life. First, I was able to take advantage of a scholarship that I had previously been awarded at MTS that would pay 40% of my tuition for my Master of Divinity, but the stipulation was I had to take at least 2 classes which I was unable to do while working full time. Secondly, our daughter became engaged several months after I retired, and she was planning a wedding for April 2010. Since she was out of the state, I was the designated venue shopper, and menu sampler along with one of her friends. Next, I was able to do something that I always wanted and that was to go on a mission trip. Therefore, in August of 2009, I went on a 9-day mission trip to Guyana, South

America. The mission trip was one of the most rewarding experiences of my life.

As I reminisce, I remember once I was having a pity party and as I sat at my desk, I said "They eliminated my job." I heard the Holy Spirit as if a person was standing in front of me talking and the voice said, "They didn't do anything, I did this for you." The Holy Spirit was accurate, I was informed by a former co-worker, 7 years later, that 2016 was the first time that the company offered another severance package and that it was not nearly as nice as what we received in 2009.

Hence, God provided just enough information and direction through the dream so that I was able to make the decision that was a part of God's plans for my life. Similarly, an example of dreams that offered guidance in Scripture is found in Matthew 2:13. An angel warned Joseph to take Mary and the child, Jesus, leave Bethlehem, and provided guidance by directing him to go to Egypt to be safe from those who sought to harm the child. Hence, in this passage, God revealed information to Joseph that pertained to his family. It is comforting and reassuring to know that God cares about concerns that we sometimes regard as insignificant in the grand scheme.

Not only can dreams provide direction, but they can also provide solace for the journey of the dreamer. In the Bible, Jacob was on his way to Haran from Beersheba when he became tired from the journey and stopped to rest. Jacob was not just tired, but fearful, lonely and depressed. He stopped short of his destination, arriving at Bethel and fell asleep. God communicated God's covenant in a dream to him. God promised to bless Jacob, his descendants and furthermore, the entire earth through Jacob and his offspring. Moreover, God would protect Jacob and bring him back to the land of his inheritance. The dream provided information and comfort for Jacob since he was far from his home (Genesis 28:10-22).

Likewise, while Zechariah was serving as priest before God in the Temple, he saw an angel in a vision who informed him that his barren wife would have a son. The angel gave Zechariah the name God had selected for his son and informed him that his son would be great in the sight of God (Luke 1:5-15). He got good news of God's plans and direction for a name.

Chapter 5

Discernment

"Once when the king of Aram was at war with Israel, he took counsel with his officers. He said, "At such and such a place shall be my camp." **9** But the man of God sent word to the king of Israel, "Take care not to pass this place, because the Arameans are going down there." **10** The king of Israel sent word to the place of which the man of God spoke. More than once or twice he warned such a place so that it was on the alert.**11** The mind of the king of Aram was greatly perturbed because of this; he called his officers and said to them, "Now tell me who among us sides with the king of Israel?" **12** Then one of his officers said, "No one, my lord king. It is Elisha, the prophet in Israel, who tells the king of Israel the words that you speak in your bedchamber." **13** He said, "Go and find where he is; I will send and seize him." He was told, "He is in Dothan." **14** So he sent horses and chariots there and a great army; they came by night, and surrounded the city.**15** When an attendant of the man of God rose early in the morning and went out, an army with horses and chariots was all around the city. His servant said, "Alas, master! What shall we do?" **16** He replied, "Do not be afraid, for there are more with us than there are with them." **17** Then Elisha prayed: "O LORD, please open his eyes that he may see." So the LORD opened the eyes of the servant, and he saw; the mountain was full of horses and chariots of fire all around Elisha" 2 Kings 6:8-17 (NRSV).

God is sovereign and does what God wants to do in the manner that God wants to do. In this section you will see how the dreams of three generations were intertwined.

Barbara's Dreams

One night early in January 2013, I (Barbara) was given in a dream the date "April 2." Immediately, I thought about our daughter, Brandi, who was scheduled to have our first grandbaby on February 28, in Key West, Florida. The thought that came to my mind was that one who specializes in Obstetrics and Gynecology (OBGYN) would not allow someone to go over a month beyond a due date. Tragically, thirty-three days after she was born, my granddaughter transitioned on the exact date that was given to me in my dream. With time and reflection, I recognized that God had provided comfort to our daughter, son-in-law, and us. The dream felt like God was telling us He was there for us and was holding all our lives in His hands.

As I grieved the loss of my grandchild, I read a book by Dr. Weems that said what I could not articulate.

I found solace as the words spoke volumes to me while I waited to hear from God about a situation that was so close to my heart.

In her book *Listening for God*, Dr. Renita J. Weems (25) stated:

> "No one is ever prepared to endure the long silence that follows intimacy...It is the hardest thing to talk about, and it is the hardest thing in the spiritual journey to prepare for. The long silence between intimacies, the interminable pause between words, the immeasurable seconds between pulses, the quiet between epiphanies, the hush after ecstasy, the listening for God—this is the spiritual journey, learning how to live in the meantime, between the last time you heard from God and the next time you hear from God."

As I reflect on the revelation of the diagnosis that was made known by the Holy Spirit in my dream was that it was Memorial Day, May 27, 2013. In the dream I heard heart myopathy. I got up and was going to research what that meant, but as soon as I crossed the threshold of my bedroom, the enemy attempted to steal the dream and I forgot what the dream was. I said God I can't remember what the dream was, and I heard the Holy Spirit say "Back up." I immediately backed up and was now back in my bedroom and I heard it again "heart myopathy." I went to the computer and googled heart myopathy and what came up was cardiomyopathy. I sent an email to Brandi believing that it would comfort her and her husband. Our daughter and son-in-law were encouraged by the dream. Three months after the dream, the autopsy was released and the diagnosis was what the Holy Spirit had provided me three months earlier in the dream. I reflected on the statement of Shawn Bolz, "when people hear that God knows precious details of their lives, whether historical or current facts, it helps them to feel known by God and cared for by him."[4]

Brandi and Braya's Dreams

We serve an awesome God who continues to amaze us. God gave a little bit of information to both

[4] Shawn Bolz, Translating God Hearing God For Yourself And The World Around You, (Glendale: ICreate Productions, 2015), 103.

mom and I for the journey ahead. In January 2013 God gave mom the date of April 2, although she did not know want it meant. I remember it was a few days after my first child was born in February 2013, I dreamed that she passed away, but I clearly heard a voice in the dream that said she would not make it, but the others would. As you can imagine this dream was very upsetting, and I felt completely helpless. In April 2013, my daughter passed away and I was utterly heart broken. I was angry, sad, guilty, and other countless negative emotions. I could not understand why God would show me something ahead of time that I could do nothing about. I began to feel guilty that maybe I could have done something and just did not do the right thing. I came out of the experience with a constant feeling of fear about the next bad thing that was undoubtedly around the corner. Being pessimistic seemed safer than expecting good things and being disappointed when they turn out badly. Shall we indeed accept [only] good from God and not [also] accept adversity and disaster?" Job 2:10 NIV.

In 2015, I, (Brandi) was blessed to give birth to a beautiful baby girl, Braya, but a day after she was born, she had to be airlifted to a hospital because they were concerned about something they heard with her heart. I was devastated and to make matters worse, I was not cleared to check out of the hospital and could not be with my little girl while she was in the ICU. That one dream that seemed so cruel in which God revealed the passing of one child but promised that my other children would survive was now my lifeline. It was the thing that stabilized my faith so that I knew my little girl would be fine. She was in the ICU for a week and left the hospital with a heart monitor that she wore for 3 months. But Praise God, she was cleared and no longer had to wear it. Braya is thriving, and she is a kind, loving, and healthy girl.

When Braya was 3 years old, Braya's preschool teacher and the other day care staff wished me congratulations on the baby - I was of course confused since I was not pregnant. Well, I found out that Braya was telling the entire day care that I was pregnant with her baby brother. I was embarrassed to keep having to explain to all the staff that I was not pregnant. I pulled Braya aside and asked her why she kept telling everyone that I was pregnant, and she said she dreamed that she had a baby brother.

Not too long after this, I had a dream about 4 children - two girls and two boys - playing in a room. The bedroom had twin beds in it. One of the girls and one of the boys were so energetic. The kids were jumping on the bed and just having a great time. The other two children were watching the two that were playing. When I came into the room, it was clear that I knew the two that were playing, but I did not recognize the older children. I called out Bevin's name and then both older children sat at the foot of each of the twin beds like they were sentries. I have experienced and learned much, and on the other side of the tragedy since my daughter passed, it became clear that the dream that forecasted my daughter's death would also serve as a source of comfort. I am slowly coming to accept that I could not have prevented the death of Bevin. This does not mean that I did not wish for another outcome. As I have matured, I have found comfort that God did reveal to us through His constant care and grace that nothing caught Him by surprise. I have two beautiful children physically with me that daily confirms God's love for me.

Dreams for Others

There are many experiences such as the one mentioned above by Brandi, that leads me to believe that dreams and visions are tools that can and do reveal to us the heart of God. It took me many years to understand what I know about dreams and visions, and it is a continuous learning process for me.

For example, God allowed me to contact then Presiding Elder E. Anne Henning Byfield back in 2009 or 2010, whom I knew only casually at the time. I shared with her the details of a dream that I just could not shake which God gave me about Presiding Elder and her brother, who was a Bishop in the AME Church. In the dream Bishop Henning was driving a vehicle and he picked up Elder Byfield in his vehicle. They rode together for a while and then he got out of the vehicle and she continued.

Presiding Elder Byfield was subsequently elected and consecrated as the 135th Bishop of the African Methodist Episcopal Church at the 50th Quadrennial Session of the General Conference on July 11, 2016, in Philadelphia, Pennsylvania. She was then assigned to the 16th Episcopal District of the AME Church which comprises Guyana/Suriname, Virgin Islands, European, Dominican Republic, Haiti, Jamaica, and Winward Islands. The dream confirmed what would be a historical moment in African Methodism as Bishop Byfield and her brother, Bishop Cornal Garnett Henning, Sr., served together for two years as Bishops in the African Methodist Episcopal Church before his transition on May 15, 2018.

Sometime later, Elder Byfield stated during our conversation that the dream confirmed that God had instructed her to seek episcopal office. Bishop Byfield publicly acknowledged the nature of the dream publicly on October 7, 2017, at the Ordination Service at the 143rd Session of the West Tennessee Annual Conference.

The Scriptures such as Acts 10 demonstrate that dreams have had a significant role in the emerging story of God's people. We, like the mothers and fathers of the faith, need to watch for how God uses dreams to instruct, encourage and guide us. It is my belief that it is essential for the Church to refocus and include, as it operates in the spiritual realm, dreams, and visions because individuals must be educated as to the significant role, they play in casting God's vision for the faith community. This accomplishment will occur when leadership is intentional in teaching about dreams and visions. Joel prophesied in Joel 2:28 that God's sons and daughters would prophesy, and the old men would dream dreams and young men would see visions. People who are struggling to understand their purpose and their gifts need to know that God has a plan for their lives.

However, the Church has remained silent and focused instead on Bible Study and in many instances, have omitted teaching on directing individuals to utilize the gifts of dreams and visions as a means of discerning God's will. There are dreamers and those who see visions within our congregations; however, they are unsure what to do with what God is revealing to them, do not know what to do about it; and they are afraid to share with others because they do not understand how to interpret dreams. Moreover, others are questioning if what they see is from God or is it some mystical experience they are conjuring in their subconsciousness. I admit that I am at times, hesitant and unsure on how to interpret if what I have received is from God, only for me, or if it is to be interpreted for the other person as well.

The challenge for us is that we allow our misguided ideas to overrule what we know in our heart and therefore, we rely less on the Spirit and more on what we think we know. The question we must ask is why are we reluctant to embrace dreams and visions to connect with God? Occasionally, we get our communication crossed when we are not intentionally listening to God; however, we must be receptive to whatever means God chooses to relay information to us for edification of the body of Christ. I firmly believe that since we are often distracted because of what is vying for our attention, we are not always aware that God is present; however, the time when we are asleep (and a captive audience); God is able to communicate with us on those things God wants us to know.

6

Chapter 6

Encouragement

Luke 18:1 reminds us that we should always remain prayerful. I had been wondering when I was going to be noticed for the work that I had been doing on the job. I thought to myself, "I have great work ethics, I stay away from the politics that occur in corporate America and I go beyond what is asked so that I work in a spirit of excellence." Yet still I wondered why I was not getting promoted. Psalm 138:8a in the Amplified Bible states "The LORD will accomplish that which concerns me; Your [unwavering] lovingkindness, O LORD, endures forever."

God has placed me amid individuals from different backgrounds and denominations who have provided encouragement for me in the form of prophetic words confirming what God told me that my gifts were. I am grateful to God for all who have shared a word with me.

For example, on Thursday, June 7, 2024, I was walking and listening to the book of 1 Kings on my phone Bible application. The Lord reminded me of the passage in 2 Chronicles 6:1-6 that He gave me 25 years ago and told me to find the note, which I kept among important papers, and insert in this book. I had been puzzled by the dream and was led to ask one of the managers who worked with me at International Paper, at the computer center in the operations department who had a strong prayer life to give me the interpretation. He prayed about the dream and provided me the interpretation. The interpretation of the dream he provided was "Low, I am with you always, I fulfill my promises, ESTABLISH yourself for Me so others know where I dwell. You have asked for spiritual blessings, and I will give them to you. Not only will you be filled with My Glory, you have also received My blessings. – you and your household. Continue in My work. Continue to do those things I put into your spirit. For your Spirit and My Spirit are one. Expect My blessings. Receive My blessings. I keep the promises I make. I will continue to bless you!" It has been years since I thought of that dream, but God brought it my remembrance, at a time when I needed the reassurance from God of God's purpose for my life.

Therefore, despite what we might think is insignificant, God is concerned about every aspect of our lives. Little did I know that God was working on the things that were a concern of mine. On Thursday, January 22, 2004, God revealed to me that my manager would come to my desk and ask me to dial someone on the phone. I do not recall who I was to call, but I dialed the person that I was asked to contact. At that point, my manager picked up the telephone and asked the person a question and the person either said no or the answer that my manager received was not what he expected because my manager sounded surprised. The person on the phone said my manager's name and said another position and indicated what the position level was. When I woke up, I rebuked the enemy and anything that the enemy was attempting to steal from me and thanked God for the increase. God is so faithful, on March 31, 2004, I was advised that my position had been upgraded to the position God revealed in the dream and I received a promotional increase, however the merit amount did not increase based on new salary with the promotion, which was why my manager was disappointed.

Despite how difficult the seasons are in our lives; God always has a way to encourage us to remain on the journey. It was during this time that I needed encouragement. The church was not in a good place financially. I had been at the church for a little over a year and could not see the light at the end of the tunnel.

However, on Sunday, November 12, 2006, at 5:24 am, God revealed to me in a dream that I was talking on a beige color telephone, and I had been given a huge silver bowl, the size of two serving trays. I had two bags of fruit that I was preparing to wash so that the people could eat. There was an abundance of grapes, plums and the colors were bright green and purple colors. Amidst the dream, the Lord wanted to encourage me and let me know that the ministry would be fruitful and that the people would also be blessed.

God was continuing to encourage me, on Tuesday November 21, 2006, God revealed to me in a dream that I was in a garden, no grass only small green plants and there were no weeds in the garden. Then I saw an elderly man tending the garden. I was sitting on what appeared to be a platform and the elderly man was a step lower and I was holding his right hand. I started to come down off the platform and step-down, but I did not because I was afraid that I would step on the plants. The ground was dusty, although all it needed was water. This was a great reminder that regardless of what it appeared in the natural, the current place where I was serving in ministry was fertile ground.

God knows when the next chapter in our lives will begin. God also knows how difficult it can be for us to move from our comfort zones and take a leap of faith by trusting that all things work together for good for those who will trust the prodding of the Holy Spirit. It was during such a time when this dream occurred, it was Sunday morning, July 26, 2015, at 6:00 am. God had been urging me to return to school to get my Doctor of Ministry degree. I really did not want to return to school. I thought I was through with the late-night reading of books and writing papers. I was enjoying time with my husband and traveling to see our granddaughter. Additionally, the finances of the ministry were beginning to look great. The truth is, I felt ill-equipped to be in a doctorate level program as I had the idea of a doctoral program being theologians having debates about biblical subjects. I wondered what the congregation would think about me pursuing this degree. Would the congregation think it had no value to breaking the Word down and applying it to their lives? I quickly realized that I was allowing the enemy to get in my head and attempt to talk me out of returning to school.

In the dream God allowed me to see a chasm and it appeared to be the size of interstate lanes. The lane nearest to me was rugged and I heard the Holy Spirit say, "Leap over the chasm and while leaping say in the name of Jesus." I saw my girlfriend, Carolyn Wright Singleton, on my right cheering me on, telling me that I can do it. I was afraid because I could see black sand

and the opening was deep and large. I found the strength and said, "In the name of Jesus" and as I leaped, my fingers caught the edge of the ledge. I thought that I was going to fall into the abyss, but I heard the Holy Spirit tell me to say "In the name of Jesus," so I said in the name of Jesus, and as I said that I was able to pull myself onto the ledge. Not only did I pull myself over the ledge, but I was able to stand on the ledge with my hands raised. I believe that God gave me the dream so that I would understand the power associated with the name of Jesus.

I am certain that God desired for me to grasp that what I was about to embark upon would need a leap of faith, but if I call on the name of Jesus, I will be able to stand and be victorious. On April 22, 2019, I sat before the Committee regarding my dissertation entitled "Dreams and Visions – A Means of Discernment." The presence of God was present, and the Committee stated that I only needed to make some editing corrections and return everything in two days. I was commended for presenting a project that had not been done before at MTS. I was overjoyed to hear someone refer to me as Dr. Green. When I got to my car, I raised my hands, praised, and thanked God for the journey that only God could bring me through. May 11, 2019, I walked across the stage having completed my Doctor of Ministry. On Tuesday, July 4, 2023, I spoke to my friend, Carolyn, she said she needed confirmation or affirmation that she was being used to encourage someone else in the spiritual realm.

I was feeling and uneasiness in my spirit for approximately a year and did not know if it was pertaining to the job or ministry, but I had mixed thoughts about both. God always has a plan and I believe that God wants to bring clarity during times of uncertainty. On October 27, 2005, it was during our annual conference series, God gave me a dream, and in the dream, I saw a sanctuary with red carpet and pews. Then the scenery changed, and I walked to the church with my robes in my hands. What was interesting is that I had forgotten about the dream once I journaled. God saw to assign me to another charge, and I pondered why it caught me off guard. As I pondered this new assignment, God began to reveal the dream that I received several days earlier. The dream was a wonderful confirmation that the assignment was indeed from God. Additionally, the church is a short distance from my house and therefore, the scene of me walking to the church with my robes in my hand certainly spoke to how close I lived to my assignment.

This New Testament passage in Matthew 1:18-21 is significant because it records the story of Joseph, Jesus's earthly father, and his struggle to marry Mary. Joseph was unsettled about whether he should wed Mary because she was pregnant prior to consummating their marriage. God used a dream to encourage, provide guidance, and the direction Joseph needed to marry Mary now knowing that the child was of God. Furthermore, the angel provided Joseph with information as to the child's name and the vocation of the baby.

Another example of encouragement in visions comes from Judges 7:13-15. This story has always amazed me because it reveals that God will use whomever God desires to fulfil the plan that God has for our lives. In the passage God encouraged Gideon to go to battle with 300 men by allowing a Midianite to tell his dream to his fellow Midianite friend who gave the interpretation. When Gideon overheard the dream that a loaf of barley bread tumbled into the camp and overturned the tent, he had the assurance to go to battle with 300 men. God not only provided Israel's enemy with a dream, but also provided the interpretation so that Gideon would not be intimidated by the number of the men fighting with the Midianites.

On another occasion the narrative in Genesis 40:5-13 tells of two of Pharaoh's officials, a butler and a baker, who were imprisoned during the same time as Joseph, and both were given dreams with its own personal interpretation that pertained to the individuals concerned. As illustrated in the pericope above, the dream provided revelatory information pertinent to the butler and the baker.

Chapter 7

Prayers for the Church

We are living in times when we not only need to pray for ourselves and those dear to us, but we need to intercede and pray for the Church. You will note that I said it is imperative that we pray, not for denominations, although they need our prayers. We must be intentional and pray for the body of Christ. We especially need to pray for those who are in leadership positions.

Dreams and visions for me connects me to intercessory prayer and I believe that if a person has a strong prayer life and study of the Word it can assist in discerning God's will for their lives or others. For example, it is frequently as I am in prayer and struggling with several passages for preaching, God will give a dream confirming the passage I am to preach. Or if I am struggling with a decision, the answer often will be revealed in a dream.

On Sunday, September 1, 2012, at 6:00 am, God showed me Reverend LaWanda Denise Pope standing at an easel designing the cover for a children's book. It was just beautiful. The drawing looked as if it was designed with a pencil, then when I looked closely, it was completely without color. The design had a charcoal look, there were 3 stick children, but they had hair and it resembled 2 boys and a girl. It was the kind of picture that resembled children and that the book was written for children. There was handwriting at the top and a picture on the bottom, although I could not recall what the picture was. I contacted Reverend Pope on September 2, and she confirmed that she had the cover design for her book, and it was exactly as God had given me in the dream. I believe the dream meaning was two-fold. It was a means of encouragement for Reverend LaWanda to remind her that God had indeed called her to write a book. Additionally, it was for me to pray for the Church and the blessings that will come forth because of the book.

What are Intercessory Prayer and Dreams?

I believe the clearest definition for intercessory prayer is found in the Bible. "And I sought for anyone among them who would repair the wall and stand in the breach before me on behalf of the land, so that I would not destroy it; but I found no one" (Ezekiel 22:30 NRSV). In the passage mentioned above, God brought a charge against all of God's people. The indictment was against both the leadership and the common people in Jerusalem. The prophets and the princes fleeced the vulnerable for corrupt profit. And the priests, who were the spiritual leaders, violated the law because they overlooked the difference concerning the sacred and the common. Consequently, the Lord sought for someone to intercede on behalf of the people so that the city would not be destroyed, but God could not find anyone.

The Apostle Paul urged the believers in 1 Timothy 2:1 to offer supplications, prayers, intercessions, and thanksgivings be made for everyone. The etymology of the word "intercession" is derived from the Latin *inter*, meaning "between" and *cedere*, meaning "to go." Jesus told his disciples a parable about their need to pray and never lose heart.

There might be someone saying how will I find time to pray with all that is required of me and there are only 24 hours a day, and yes, I do require sleep. I remember years ago, I thought that I had to be sitting or kneeling to pray and then it was revealed to me that if I waited to sit and kneel during the day, I might not ever get an opportunity to pray. That is when the revelation came to me that I could be going about my daily routine and pray at the same time. Intercessory prayer is not necessarily about the physical posture during prayer but it about the consciousness that we are in the presence of God when we pray.

It is my belief that for me there is a connection between intercessory prayer, discernment, and understanding God's will through dreams and visions. As individuals we are led to intercede on behalf of ourselves, our families, colleagues, other leaders, and parishioners. Therefore, based upon what was revealed in a dream or vision could perhaps prevent many of the self-destructive actions that are occurring in our society. It is also my point of view that if individuals know that they are being prayed for, they will perhaps realize how important they are that someone was willing to offer on their behalf, prayers, supplications, petitions to God so that the will of God for their lives will be accomplished.

Furthermore, although all believers are called to intercede on behalf of others, there seems to be individuals who have a calling to pray as they are content praying for longer periods of times. Additionally, the individuals mentioned above also seem to have a greater percentage of their prayers answered. I knew that I had an intercessory prayer calling upon my life, however, it was not until I was introduced to the book *Could You Not Tarry One* Hour by Larry Lea (50) and the promise God made to him that praying for at least an hour "something supernatural will happen in your life" (Lea). For this reason, I felt drawn to the promise, and I felt God shifting me to devote more time to prayer and sensed being led to tithe my prayer time. Therefore, I began to spend a minimum of 10 percent of my day in prayer and meditation. When I think of biblical characters who prayed frequently, there are several people who come to mind. For example, Moses was called to lead the children of Israel from bondage and was constantly praying for them. Anna was an 84-year-old widow who was always at the Temple. The Scripture states she worshipped God by fasting and praying day and night. The prophet Samuel was also a great intercessor. According to the Scripture 1 Samuel 15:35, when God no longer had faith in Saul, Samuel continued to pray for him. Intercessory prayer can lead into warfare prayer depending on what God reveals. Ephesians 6:10-17 admonishes us to put on the whole armor of God. For example, I have been to countries in my dreams that I have not physically visited or been given names and faces of people I have never met but know that I am to pray for them and the Church of God.

For example, I had two dreams on May 22, 2019, this is the second dream. God revealed at 6:00 am that Reverend Joy W. Yancy was leading a dance ministry, like Dance the Word Ministry at St. Andrew where she was a dance member. It seemed as if all the persons in the ministry were men. One of her parishioners, Sister Sandra Bradley was beside Reverend Joy as she was dancing, they were so happy. They were both dressed in white. I was talking to someone and said she was an intercessor, and she was doing for Reverend Joy what my armorbearer does for me. I was wearing purple with a purple doctoral hood in my hand. Someone was complimenting me on the hood being so beautiful along with other complimentary things, but I can't recall all of it. Sister Sandra had Reverend Joy's robe in her hand. It was as if Reverend Joy had the robe on over her white skirt and top but took it off to dance and Sister Bradley had put the robe up.

I spent some time in prayer to get the interpretation and this is what I received: Sister Bradley is called to be Reverend Joy's armorbearer. Secondly, it seemed as if Reverend Joy is wanting to start a ministry with the men; not sure if dance or what. I received confirmation from Reverend Joy, she wanted to apply for a Center for Faith and Imagination grant (CFI) from Memphis Theological Seminary to begin a Creative Careers Outreach Ministry. I urged Reverend Joy to complete the application, because I believed God was giving her success with the grant. Early fall, 2019, Reverend Joy was one of the first of CFI Fellows.

Moreover, Reverend Joy asked me to function as her CFI Colleague in her Fellowship. Additionally, on Saturday, February 1, 2020, I received a text message from Reverend Joy confirming that "Sandra Bradley is her armorbearer. However, our formal pastor/armorbearer relationship never had a chance to develop as less than two months later we were impacted by the pandemic."

None of these women (Reverend Joy nor Phoebee mentioned below) came to me however, God knew that they were in need of prayer, and I was available, so God used me to relay messages of encouragement which not only blessed them, but the body of Christ. While I am unsure of what was occurring in the spiritual realm during the early hours of May 22, 2019, it is evident that God wanted intercession to take place. Both dreams were concerning clergy persons who are bi-vocational and hold positions of leadership in ministry and in their secular jobs.

This is another example of what I described. The names in this dream have been changed to protect the identity and privacy of those in the dream. This was the first dream that I had on Wednesday, May 22, 2019, at 6:00 am. God revealed what Phoebe was wearing along with a detailed description of the woman, her hairstyle, and her attire. It appeared that Phoebe was talking to someone trying to get them to understand something, but the individual appeared to be in a bad place spiritually.

I had been praying about the dream and at 6:16 am, I texted Phoebe and informed her that God continued to drop her in my spirit. I said God can handle whatever you are struggling with that has your mind so confused and I ended the text with "I'm praying for you!" Phoebe texted me at approximately 10:06 am and said "Good morning! Thanks, for the prayers, but I do not know that I'm struggling with anything, but I will definitely start seeking God for answers." I was so confident of what God had revealed to me in the dream that at approximately 3:11 pm, I texted Phoebe, sent her what I had written in my journal of the dream and said "You were wearing a dark colored dress. It seemed like it was black, white and grey. You were trying to explain or get a woman to understand what you were saying. The person had a short natural hair style, but the person did not seem to want to listen to what you were saying, and you grew frustrated."

At 4:36 pm, Phoebe responded and said "Wow. That might be the new person on the team. The person has been here since last July, but is not comprehending at all, constantly making huge mistakes and never wants to own up to anything. The employee has caused so much dissension in the workplace. Your description is almost perfect. Wow, I know God has you definitely interceding for me." Phoebe stated "Nobody but God could have revealed that to you. Glory and praise God! I am over here shouting and in tears. Thanks so much!"

On the morning of February 8, 2021, at 6:48 am God revealed Reverend Dr. Sarita Wilson-Anderson to me in a dream. Dr. Sarita was smiling and standing in a room with books in her hands. The room was clean, it appeared to be a library or office with lots of wall bookcases. Everything was labeled and in order. She was wearing an olive green either dress or top, I could only see from waist upward. She was holding either folders or binders to her chest as she was looking around and smiling.

As I prayed about the dream, God provided the interpretation by allowing me to know that Dr. Sarita was serene and that everything was in order. I thought about the dream several times and felt as though God was leading me to share with Dr. Wilson-Anderson. I texted the dream to Dr. Sarita on February 9, 2021, at 8:33 pm. She immediately responded at 8:41 pm and said and I quote "Amen. I love books. I purchase more than I can read. I love rooms with wall bookcases. I received every bit of this!!! Thank you!" "Wow! I actually had on a green dress yesterday! God's gifts are so amazing!"

I was a delegate to the 51st Session of the AME General Conference which was held in Orlando, Florida. I arrived in Orlando on Friday, July 2, 2021. I had been in prayer for several weeks asking God to allow me to spend quality time in prayer and reading the Word while on the trip since I would be traveling alone. On Monday, July 5, 2021, at 6:00 am, God revealed to me that I was in a church and a clergy friend who has since transitioned came to me and said for me to pray and said the names of two pastors in the Conference that I was to undergird in prayers. In the dream, I began to pray and plead the blood of Jesus. I said, "God I say what you say about the situation." I partially quoted Job 22:26-28 when we delight in the Almighty and lift our face verse 27 states if I pray to God and God will hear me and I pay my vows (praise and worship), verse 28 then I will decide and decree a thing and it shall be established for me and the delight of God's favor will shine upon my ways.

Additionally, God provided the interpretation of the dreams and I shared with both individuals, who were encouraged by the dream. One of the Pastors even noted that the Scripture I quoted in the dream was what she had been doing "declaring and decreeing."

Chapter 8
Testimonies

So far, the focus of this text has been on the potential value of a dream or vision interpretation. There is, however, another value which is the sharing of dream experiences as a testimony of faith. The shared personal spiritual experience of one person with others allows a person to be open to possibilities that they never thought possible. For example, it was during the fall of 1984, shortly after my call into the ministry while we were living in Flanders, New Jersey, God spoke to me. The scenery was the basement of Bethel AME Church in Boonton, New Jersey, God spoke to me through the wind. In the dream, God revealed that I along with other members were sitting and the basement door was open, and suddenly, I heard the wind and then the voice asked, "Is there a Bible in the house?" I looked around and wondered why all the people were in the building and no one was responding. They were sitting and standing around as if they had not heard anyone speak. The voice was much sterner the second time, asking "Is there a Bible in the house?" I reached for the Bible and the voice said, "Teach My Word and preach My Word."

I realized later that no one responded because although there were others in the dream, God was speaking directly to me. This is the second dream that confirmed the order of my calling. In the first dream, Jesus walked me to the pulpit of the church and said, "Teach My Word and preach My Word." That is exactly how my ministry began. I began teaching St. James AME's Bible Study prior to Reverend Shirley Owens Prince leaving to become a preacher on the staff of Mississippi Boulevard Christian Church. In 1990, I was licensed to preach in the AME Church and preached my first sermon entitled "An Encounter with the Sprint Giver," taken from John 4:7-38. I have shared this dream numerous times and the response is along the line, wow, God does use unusual methods to communicate with us. I don't think that we encourage each other enough to be receptive to the countless ways in which God speaks to others. We perhaps shy away from sharing our experiences, not realizing that those encounters give confidence to others and their faith walks with the Lord. Such was the case for those at St. James that mentioned that they knew the Bible Study was under good leadership and because of the testimony, they had first-hand knowledge that God had predetermined the person to take over the Bible Study years before Minister Prince went to Mississippi Boulevard Christian Church.

As I stated previously, my dream life and my prayer life are intertwined. In 2007, I was asked to preach at a prayer breakfast. I was going through a time when I was trying to work through some past hurt. I was struggling because I did not want to bleed upon the people, therefore, I did not necessarily want to take the assignment. The person who asked me to preach was adamant that she had heard from God, and I was the only individual who God gave as the preacher. However, I did not want to be disobedient and said, "God if you are wanting me to do this, then, send me on a fast." God did and I went on a 7 day fast and food never crossed my mind. As I spent much time in reading and praying about what to do, God gave me a dream and, in the dream, the voice said, "I want you to know what the enemy thinks of you." I saw myself at the altar on my knees in the church where I was asked to preach, and there was a sign on my back. The words were written on a white paper with black letters, it said "The **B***** is praying."

For that reason, this dream was extremely impactful because I have asked God countless times, "Do my prayers make a difference?" Now I am confident that my prayers are, in fact, an irritant to the enemy and I am even more determined to intercede on behalf of others!

On August 30, 2015, at 4:45 am God revealed to me in a dream that I was in a presidential suite. It seemed as if I was in the same place where President Obama and First Lady were staying. I asked why they were staying at this location, and someone said they were staying there because they were getting the White House ready for the incoming President. The person said it is customary that they incoming president will stay at another hotel in the presidential suite until the White House is cleaned. I thought the dream was odd because the Obamas were already living in the White House.

It was my desire to visit the White House for our anniversary in September 2015, but we did not submit the background check until early August, and unfortunately, we did not get a response on our background check. I was disappointed and thought perhaps we would try again for our anniversary in September 2016. I had begun researching hotels in proximity to the White House. Interestingly, I found a place called the AKA White House and thought it would be great. On November 6, 2015, we were blessed to have a granddaughter born in Key West, FL and late November 2015, the Lord dropped in my spirit to talk to my husband and then contact our daughter to see if she and her family would like to take a family trip to Washington, DC to visit the White House in April. Everyone was excited and our daughter said it would be great because our granddaughter would be 6-months old and a good age to travel. For this trip to become a reality, we needed to submit our request for the White House visit at the same time so that the background check could be completed together. We were allowing 4-5 months for everything to get approved. Then, January 18, 2016, at 7:30 am, God gave me revelation that we would be staying in the Penthouse at the AKA White House Hotel in Washington, DC which is like a presidential suite. I was believing God for the trip. Although, we did not go to Washington, DC in September 2015, God had something greater planned.

It did happen, Arch, Brandi, Brandon, Braya, and I stayed at the AKA White House arriving April 25 and departing April 30, 2016. The hotel was only 3 blocks from the White House. I had no idea that God was preparing to give me the desire of my heart for the trip to Washington, DC. I am learning how to interpret what God is revealing and it is amazing for me to think that

God cares so much for us that God will give us a glimpse into what will be manifested. The hotel had made major renovations; therefore, the dream was revealing that the Penthouse would be like a presidential suite and that the hotel name was the connection to the White House and all within walking distance. It was a wonderful trip, and we took a lot of pictures of the hotel, and at the White House a couple was kind enough to take a family picture of us on the steps of the White House.

In another instance, God gave me a vision on July 12, 2020, at 10:30 pm., I was at home, I was not asleep, I closed my eyes and God revealed to me that Jolena Brown was wearing a wedding dress and was expecting a baby. I had forgotten about the dream and then on December 31, 2020, the Holy Spirit reminded me of the dream, and I sent a text message to her revealing what God had given to me.

Jolena's responded on January 1, 2021, stating that she and her husband wanted a baby, but conception had not happened yet. I responded by saying that God is able and for them to begin to thank God for entrusting a child into their care. Additionally, I told her to begin to ask God to give life to she and her husband's love and that I would be praying for them. I was led to ask them to read Exodus 23:25-26 in the Contemporary English Version.

Jolena noted that she had the Scripture in the bathroom mirror and read it each time she looked up and saw it. I was led to order the book "The Power of a Parent's Blessing," by Craig Hill and they received it on January 6, 2021.

On September 8, 2021, I received great news. God is indeed faithful; Jolena and her husband were expecting a baby girl to be born in January of 2022. The baby girl was born on December 31, 2021.

Still another instance in June 2022, God will use what one would think to be a desperate situation and get the glory, involved an incident with a contractor where we were on the verge of losing a large sum of money. I was somewhat anxious because we had made arrangements and had contacted the bishop to come to consecrate and dedicate the building and parking lot. It was a major effort that we had in the works and needed this check and the parking lot to be paved. I prayed and asked some prayer warriors to stand with me and the Trustees as I brought the matter to God's remembrance that the church had been faithfully tithing on all income received by the church since March 2020. I reminded God that we had given cheerfully, not grudgingly nor of necessity, but that we were cheerful givers. I asked God not to let the devil steal our money and reminded God of the Word that stated if we were obedient and brought the tithe into the storehouse, God, You said You would rebuke the devourer for our sakes.

On Sunday, July 3, 2022, I woke up at 5:45 am and prayed and fell back asleep and was dreaming, when I woke up at 6:00 am I was singing the song, "God Never Fails," the lyrics that I was singing in the dream was "keep the faith, never cease to pray, morning, noon, and night. Just walk upright, for God never fails." I woke up and googled the words to the song since it had been 15 or more years since I last heard the song. Here is a portion of the song "He abides with me, and He gives me victory: "God never fails, if you can keep the faith and never cease to pray, call Him noon day or night and He will be there. You don't have to worry because God Never Fails." Several days later, we received a check.

It did not require much for me to interpret the dream. The dream encouraged me, and I felt in my spirit that everything was going to be fine. Since it was not a cashier's check, I checked the online bank for at least four (4) days to ensure that the check did clear. I praise God, for "God Never Fails."

Chapter 9

Strategies for Interpreting Dreams

Elihu, one of Job's friends, rebukes Job in the passage of Scripture found in Job 33:14-15 (KJV) "In a dream, in a vision of the night, when deep sleep falleth upon men, in slumberings upon the bed; then he openeth the ears of men, and sealeth their instruction." Elihu advises us that God gives us instructions; however, the instructions come to us in the form of dreams. We do not always understand these instructions because they are sealed. When I implemented my D.Min., project, it involved examining dreams and visions in community as a tool for discerning the will of God.

As we spend time in the presence of God, we are better equipped to discern if what was revealed to us is to be taken exactly as revealed or if implied. In Ezekiel 37:1-14 the prophet reports being transported by the Spirit of God into the valley of dry bones. What Ezekiel underwent was both visionary and symbolic. God revealed to Ezekiel the condition of the nation. However, the Sovereign God was able and was going to resurrect the nation and give new life.

Additionally, in the story recorded in Genesis 41:17-36, Pharoah king of Egypt had two dreams that were similar and inquired of Joseph for the interpretation. The first dream, he dreamed that seven fat cows were grazing along the riverbank and seven skinny cows came out of the river. The seven skinny cows devoured the seven fat cows, but the skinny cows were still skinny. The second dream of the king involved seven heads of grain on one stalk, all seven heads were plump and full. Seven withered and thin heads came out of the plump stalk and consumed the plump, full stalk. Joseph informed the king that both dreams were the same, God was warning of imminent famine that would take place.

The king trusted Joseph's interpretation because Joseph had a track record of accurately interpreting dreams. Likewise, when individuals are comfortable with a person, they will share a dream that they have dreamed. In my personal experiences, not everyone will accept revelations you have received concerning the dream they revealed and may even shy away from you. Furthermore, it is important to be sensitive to the Spirit of God as it pertains to what is to be shared when interpreting dreams. Perhaps, Joseph should have been more sensitive on how he shared his dreams with his brothers.

From my personal perspective, I believe that to hear from God, we must be led by the Holy Spirit and that is only possible as we are drawn into the presence of God by the grace of God. While hearing from God requires one to be in communion with God, it is my belief that it is almost impossible to discern if a dream or vision is from God without having a consistent, disciplined prayer life and study of the holy writ as a regular part of their personal spiritual discipline.

It is my theological assumption that although we receive dreams and visions, there must be a way in which we discern dreams and visions, since not all dreams are from God. Some dreams are demonic, some of the results from our flesh, our own thoughts and are certainly not messages from God. Therefore, we must rely upon the Holy Spirit and the Word of God as a guide. Dreams, like other fodder for discernment, should be considered within the context of community whether that representation of community is a few trusted family and friends, or the whole congregation.

Additionally, I have noticed that when I am well rested, I am able to remember more details of my dreams and better able to discern with more clarity the interpretation given. An example of a dream that requires divine insight is found in Daniel 2:1-19. One night king Nebuchadnezzar had a frightening dream that he could not remember upon awakening. He contacted the magicians, astrologers, and sorcerers, and informed them that he had a dream and demanded they tell him what he dreamed. If they were able to tell him what was dreamed, they would be honored, if not they would be killed, and their homes destroyed.

The individuals were dumbfounded as the astrologers noted no such demand has ever been made and said to the king no person living is able to provide such information, only the gods. In the meantime, the king was furious and ordered that all the wise men in Babylon, along with Daniel and his friends to be executed. When the chief executioner came to kill Daniel, he inquired why the king was so angry. Once Daniel was informed of the situation, he was taken to the king and asked the king to give him time and he would give the interpretation. Daniel went home and told his three friends about the situation and asked them to pray to the God of heaven for mercy so that they would not be destroyed with the wise men of Babylon. God honored the prayer request of Daniel and his friends, and God revealed to Daniel in a vision that night the dream and the interpretation.

Moreover, in the pericope in John 16:1-15 Jesus speaks to His disciples about the promise of the Holy Spirit. In verse 13, Jesus informs the disciples that when the Spirit of Truth comes, He will guide them to all truth for the Spirit will not speak on His own, but only what He hears from His Father. The Holy Spirit is vital as the Spirit can provide insights that we would otherwise not know, "Call to Me and I will answer you, and tell you [and even show you] great and mighty things, [things which have been confined and hidden], which you do not know *and* understand *and* cannot distinguish" (Jeremiah 33:3 AMP). I have experienced that if we pray and ask God to reveal to us what is unknown, God will do just that.

Chapter 10

The Importance of Journaling

One should not underestimate the importance of recording what has been revealed by God. In my immaturity, I did not always value what God had given me with dreams and visions. At times, I may have as many as 5-6 detailed dreams per night and because of the length of time that it took to record them, I often nixed it off and said I work on a job, I do not have 2-3 hours in the morning to record dreams.

I have repented, and many times I thought about the possible answers that were missed that would have assisted me in the areas of: my personal life, the life of others, and the ministry. I wondered how many times God was encouraging me or warning me of things to occur, but because I was disobedient and immature, I missed them. But praise be to God for God's faithfulness. In 2015 God told me to purchase a cell phone with note capability, so I purchased a Samsung Galaxy 9 which allowed me to talk and record my dreams. It reduced my journaling time. I thank God that now I faithfully record my dreams. Some of the methods which could be utilized as recording mechanisms are tablets, cell phones, actual paper journals, tape recorders, or computers.

Someone might be thinking, what does journaling have to do with dreams? It is biblical to journal "In the first year of King Belshazzar of Babylon, Daniel had a dream and visions of his head as he lay in bed. Then he wrote down the dream." You can also encourage yourself by journaling because you can confirm what God has said or done when the enemy begins to speak to you (Daniel 7:1 NRSV).

Journaling will reveal a pattern and help the dreamer with symbols to assist in interpreting future dreams. Journaling will cause you to seek God in prayer about what you have dreamed. Journaling enlarges your prayers in life so that you pray about things you would not ordinarily pray about. Journaling ensures that you are in a safe place when revealed intimate details of dreams. Sometimes, dreams are not to be shared with anyone, but for us to simply pray about what we see.

There are several advantages of writing down one's dreams and visions. First, journaling is a way in which to record so that we can determine the accuracy of what is being revealed. Often, we will not recall some details of dreams or vision if wc have not written them down. It has been said that most dreams are forgotten if not recorded within an hour of awakening. Secondly, because journaling involves body and mind, it engages new senses in our discernment process. Third, the writing process itself can help focus our meditation so we are clearer about the meaning and purpose of the dream.

Additionally, journaling can be a source of encouragement in difficult times as one can review their track record with God and how God spoke previously. Finally, I believe that taking the time to write down dreams and visions, can demonstrate to God that we value what God has revealed. As I had mentioned previously, I have periodically wondered how much I missed of what God said to me simply because I failed to take the time to jot it down.

What Should I include in My Journaling?

A journal entry is utilized to recapture the dream. It should contain as much information as you can recall. Include any notes you have about dates or numbers. Include where you were, the time of the day, and the season. Write down how you felt in the dream. Note colors, and sounds. Did anything stand out as more important in the images?

If people were in the dream, who were they and what are their relationships to you? What were their moods, what were they doing and wearing? Where were you and how did you engage with the people or objects in the dream? Were you participating or observing what was occurring? Here is an example of what a journal entry would entail:

The dream was about being in a large, beautiful room. I was attending a conference out of town and went to bed at 10:00 pm after spending time in prayer and reading the Bible. Although I was out of town and in a strange city, when I woke up from this dream, I felt relaxed. The most vivid portion of the dream that stood out were the warm colors. It seemed like things were unusually yellow and the room appeared to have a glow.

After your recording of details, also, note anything that occurred during the day that would have affected what you dreamed. How did you feel when you woke up? Were you relaxed, tense, or afraid? Any small item or feeling can be important as you sift the dream's meaning in a prayerful posture.

Finally, our closing thoughts are that we believe that the God of all creation, the Creator God continues to create dreams and visions and is revealing to those whom God chooses. It is our prayer that this book will encourage those who read and may have never had someone to affirm that God does speak to us by dreams and visions even in 2024.

From the Authors

It is with profound gratitude that we pen this note thanking you for purchasing our book. It has been 4 years in the making, but the time has come.

We pressed our way forward, although we have experienced a myriad of emotions from happiness to sadness, good health to sudden illness. However, what has been clear since the inception, is this book was not only for us but you and yours as well.

It is our prayer that you are blessed by this book and will share it with others.

Thank you, Rosetta, for years of patiently waiting for the finished product. Additionally, I thank you for the constant reminder that the book will be published in God's timing.

A special thanks is sent to the formatting team on this project, along with our prayer that God will bless you. It is because you went above and beyond your assignment, that we were able to get this book into the hands of God's people as orchestrated by God.

Blessings and love,

Brandi & Barbara
Brandi & Barbara